# Postmarked Heaven

# Postmarked Heaven

Jack Cavanaugh

Fleming H. Revell
A Division of Baker Book House Co
Grand Rapids, Michigan 49516

Published by Fleming H. Revell
a division of Baker Book House Company
P.O. Box 6287, Grand Rapids, MI 49516-6287

Printed in the United States of America

**Library of Congress Cataloging-in-Publication Data**

Cavanaugh, Jack.
    Postmarked heaven / Jack Cavanaugh.
        p.     cm.
    ISBN 0-8007-5830-7 (pbk.)
    1. Future life—Fiction. 2. Heaven—Fiction. I. Title.
PS3553 .A965 P67 2002
813′ .54—dc21                        2002002500

For current information about all releases from Baker Book House, visit our web site:
                http://www.bakerbooks.com

"Behold now the kingdom,
See with new eyes."

John Michael Talbot and Terry Talbot

# Contents

## Glimpses of Heaven

## Preparing to Come Home

# Acknowledgments

The following pages reflect many stories of historical believers present and past, brothers and sisters in the Lord, to whom I am indebted. First, for inspiring me personally by the faithfulness of their Christian walk in this troubled world; and second, for the privilege of telling their stories. I do so in the hope that God will be glorified by the telling as much as He was by the actual events.

Specifically, I want to thank evangelist Dennis F. Kinlaw for his sermon on John 18 that I heard on audio cassette. It served as the inspiration behind the letter "Malchus's Ear."

And to Raymond Davis for his wonderful book, *Fire on the Mountains*, which tells the inspiring story of the Ethiopian revival in the Wallamo province. The setting and events of this historical revival provided the background and events for my fictional character Shankala.

# We Are Aware
# of Your Struggles

# Postmarked Heaven
## Jared

Jared O'Conner, a disciple of the Lord God by the will of God, according to the promise of life that is Christ Jesus.

To the saints of earth, our dear friends and coworkers. Grace to you, and peace and mercy in abundance from God our Father and the Lord Jesus Christ.

Because of the unusual nature of our initial contact with you, we thought it best to employ a familiar form of salutation, one taken from letters old and precious. Since there's really no way to ease into it, I'll state the matter bluntly: I'm writing to you from the afterlife. I passed through the veil into the undiluted Kingdom on November 2, 2000, after thirty-one years of life on earth.

I know what you're thinking. No, this is not a prank.

Is our contacting you so hard to believe? Communication between the Kingdom and earth is transacted every day. Prayers from you, whispers of encouragement from us. And then there's the whole angelic realm. God has been using angels to serve as his messengers since the Creation.

(Let me make one thing clear from the start, though. The difference between angelic messages and these letters is that we do not speak for God. It's important that you understand that. The things we write are our own thoughts penned in our own words.)

"Why this form of communication and why now?"

Good question.

I would answer simply, "Time is short and God has granted the use of these letters for your growth in grace in consideration of the coming trial."

Maybe it would help if I told you how this whole thing came about. We were eating around the banquet table. (We do that a lot here.) As usual, the mood was festive. Talk turned to absent family members, those of you who have yet to come home. Then, my good friend Alex (you don't know him) began reminiscing about the time he sent his son off to college in a foreign country. He was struck by the similarities of that event and our relationship with you.

Like his son, you are far from home and you have relatives and friends who care deeply about you. Like his son, you are living among a people who have different values and customs, some of which are contrary to the values of your native land. And, like his son, someday you'll be returning home.

Alex remembered how one night these thoughts weighed on him. So he sat down and penned a letter to his boy. In it, he said,

First of all, son, I want you to know how much your mother and I love you. You are our child, and nothing will ever change that. Son, don't forget who you are. We raised you to fear God and live by Christian standards. Be proud of your upbringing. Never forget what we

14

taught you. We look forward to the day when we can once again see you and tell you these things face-to-face.

I don't remember whose idea it was after that, but someone said, "Wouldn't it be great if we could write such a letter to our loved ones still on earth?"

And that's how the idea was born.

Suddenly, an angel appeared with a message from Father. He liked our plan.

What's more, Father sanctioned our idea by granting four of us the privilege of writing letters to you who are still on earth.

As you might expect, many volunteered to perform this task. Four were chosen. I can't tell you what a privilege it is for me to be counted among the four.

I close this first letter with an observation that was expressed at the banquet. I share it up front because it's possibly our chief concern for you.

Having experienced life on both sides of the veil, it is generally agreed among us that the greatest challenge of living on earth is one of perception. On earth, the physical reality of the world appears to be true, while the things of the Kingdom, in comparison, lack substance and appear dreamlike.

This is the great deception, promoted by the deceiver himself. The false perception of true value accounts for more errors in judgment than any other single cause. We write to dispel this misconception. Compared to life in the Kingdom, life on earth is a vapor, a mist, smoke and mirrors. Of the two realms, God's Kingdom is more real than earth ever was or ever will be. Keep this in mind as you read these letters.

Your brother beyond the veil,
Jared

# We're Not Angels
## Dr. Everett Parker

Beloved,

Let's get one thing clear from the outset. We're not angels. Guardian or otherwise. We're beings like you. Our appointed task is to guide and console those of you who still live beyond the veil.

In the days when I was clothed in flesh, I was a physician. My name is Everett Parker. I lived most of my previous life in Cairo, Illinois, during the time of the great conflagration between the Northern and Southern states. On October 4, 1868, I died of heart failure and went on to my eternal reward. It is from here, in heaven, that I write you.

I concede such correspondence is unusual and will be treated with skepticism. Had someone told me they'd received a letter from heaven, as a physician I'd have consigned them to a mental ward, had the institutions not already been crowded with senators, congressmen, and Northern generals. (Forgive me, political humor is a difficult habit to break.)

So then, why this form of communication and why now? You're not going to like the answer.

As prophesied, the days are going to grow longer, the suffering greater, the temptations more alluring. The great falling away time is at hand. Jared alluded to this in his previous post. These letters are intended for your benefit as you prepare to face the trials of earthly existence.

And so it has fallen upon me to introduce to you the four who will be penning these letters. We thought it might be beneficial to you to hear from those of us who have experienced the human condition on earth. Each one of us has traversed the land of tears and has entered the undiluted glory that has been set aside for us.

We are the cloud spoken of in the Holy Scriptures. *Wherefore seeing we also are compassed about with so great a cloud of witnesses* (Heb. 12:1). Think of us as a presence covering the entire visible space of the heavens, without definite form but with a definite interest. Another way to think of us is in keeping with the Scripture that follows—*let us run with patience the race that is set before us*. We are the spectators in the encircling tiers of the great arena; but not spectators only, we are runners who have preceded you in the race. We have run our course and handed the baton of the Christian faith to you to finish the race. We cheer with lively interest for your success.

Among this great cloud are four of us who have been given a new voice with which to cheer you, and I am one of them. The others are Theodora, a remarkable young lady of great courage; Shankala, a tender-hearted mother who knew great suffering; and Jared O'Conner,

17

a young man with a sharp mind and keen wit. Each of these saints in the Lord will speak to you in turn, addressing the concerns of their hearts, hoping to encourage you to stay the course with their advice. Listen to them. Weigh their words. Grasp those that contain the heaviness of value with a grip commensurate to that value. Those that don't apply, pass along to others who might profit from their insights.

One thing more. I would be remiss if I did not share with you this final thought. Our participation is not without cost. Memories of life beyond the veil are disturbing and unpleasant to us. Here, the pain has been stripped away and all that remains is how God is glorified through our former suffering.

However, for us to communicate effectively with you, it is needful for us to revisit the pain of our former lives. In essence, to reopen old wounds. Not until you reach this place will you fully understand the discomfort of which I speak. It is simply enough for you to know this: We have chosen the pain that you might profit and that God be glorified afresh.

A servant of the Almighty,
Everett Parker, M.D.

# My Story
## Theodora

Beloved,

Grace and peace. Dr. Parker has already told you about the great falling away that is approaching. At his suggestion, allow me to introduce myself by telling you my story. My name is Theodora, and the days I lived beyond the veil were a time of intense persecution.

I was born and raised in Antioch, a jewel in the crown of the Roman Empire. It was said that Constantinople had finer walls and Rome a more illustrious history, but when citizens of these cities needed to relax and enjoy life, they journeyed to Antioch for its mild climate, cosmopolitan setting, and its world-renowned boulevard that was lined with columns so tall local legend insisted the firmament rested upon them.

Antioch was a treasure chest of life experiences—rich in orchards, fields, and forests; plentiful in fruit, vegetables, wheat, and timber; and abundant in fish, because we were situated within miles of the Great Sea. Every morning we filled our earthenware jars to the brim with fresh water from the public fountains. Philosophers and orators and preachers graced the steps of our buildings. Merchants and soldiers, actors and artisans, saints and missionaries walked our streets.

The church at Antioch boasted a proud heritage. Nicholas, one of our founders, was among the men chosen by the apostles to serve tables and minister to widows. It was in Antioch that the early disciples began preaching to the nations as well as to the Jews. A great many people came to the Lord in those days.

The apostles Barnabas and Paul walked our streets. For a year they taught in our churches and preached from the steps of our public buildings. It was here that the word *Christian* was coined to describe believers. Our church rested upon the spiritual foundation that was built by Niger, and Lucius, and Manean, and Bishop Ignatius, great men all. We grew up hearing the stories of how these men met persecution and death with a strength that comes through faith.

So why were we surprised when years later we too were put to the test?

Decius was emperor. He penned an edict calling upon every citizen to return to the state religion under threat of the severest of penalties. As you would expect, word of the edict spread like fire among the churches. We knew exactly what it meant. Caesar or Christ. We would be called to choose between them publicly. The local authorities began a campaign designed to pressure the citizens of Antioch to conform to the emperor's edict.

Church members began feeling the pressure immediately. Fortunatus had his lands confiscated; Apelles

20

was tortured; Patrobas was sent into exile; Babylas, an officer of the church, was killed as an example to us all.

Early on there were many who succumbed to the threats; some by making the required sacrifice to the gods, insisting they did so only with their lips and not their hearts, others by bribing officials and obtaining false certificates.

Then there were those who, in their enthusiasm to proclaim their faith, rushed to the prisons and tribunals, hoping to become fellow-sufferers with Christ and obtain a martyr's crown. Still others fled their homes to escape judgment. Among them, we learned, was the bishop of Carthage who was openly critical of those who were eager to die, saying that Jesus Himself did not rush to the cross and that nothing was to be gained by dying before the appointed hour. The bishop later died a martyr's death, thus proving wrong those who accused him of speaking from a coward's heart.

These were our options as I saw them: the way of betrayal, the way of deception, the way of delay, or the way of martyrdom. Until you are forced to choose one, you can never know with certainty how you will respond. One thing I learned early—in the face of the refiner's fire, all my good intentions were wax.

Didymus, a close friend of mine, fled the city on his day of summoning. There was nothing noble about his fleeing. He was afraid. His sudden disappearance touched us all.

Here was a man who had been counted among the brightest and best of our young believers. The offspring of Christian parents, he was weaned on the Scriptures. Together, we took food to the sick and distributed sandals to the needy. I fed off the strength of his humble spirit. At the age of seventeen he preached his first sermon. Here was a man who had been cut from church cloth and fashioned to be an officer and a bishop.

His cowardice was a blow to us all. Did we not have the bones of the great martyr Ignatius to inspire us? And if our best could not endure this present trial, what hope was there for the rest of us? My resolve was shifting sand.

On the day of my summoning I entertained thoughts of fleeing as the bishop of Carthage had done. Then I thought of Didymus, and the more I thought of him the angrier I became. If I fled, no one would believe I did so for noble reasons. Because of my association with Didymus the coward, they would lump me in with him. After calming down I concluded that fleeing only delayed the inevitable. I decided to take a stand for my faith at the tribunal.

Even now I find it difficult to describe to you the emotions I felt as I walked down the great colonnade for the last time. I walked alone. Both my parents died two years earlier when I was fifteen. My uncle, with whom I now lived, had purchased false certificates for his family. He offered to purchase one for me. I refused.

People with whom I did business every day greeted me with waves and smiles. As I walked I prayed for strength and, God willing, deliverance.

Upon reaching the tribunal, I was instructed to stand in a line that passed between two rows of soldiers. No one spoke. Expressions were humorless; mouths were set in a grim line.

Just ahead of me a man held two little girls by the hand. One of the girls turned to look at me. I recognized her from church. She was a twin. Her father, a quiet man, had lost his wife to fever only two months prior. I smiled at the inquisitive twin. She hid her face bashfully.

When it came his turn to face the magistrate, without hesitation the father did and said exactly what was expected of him. He was handed a certificate and told he was free to leave.

He turned and started when he recognized me.

"Their mother . . . " he mumbled.

"I know."

"They don't have anyone else to look after them."

"I know," I said.

It was my turn.

As I approached, the magistrate appeared bored. Seeing me, he sat up with new life. It didn't take long to discern the source of his newfound energy. A leer formed on his lips as he let his eyes feast on me. I was accustomed to the gazes of lustful men in the marketplace, but the sheer boldness of this man was unnerving.

"What have we here?" he said with a sugary smile.

It was sickening.

"I have come as summoned," I said. This was my moment of truth. I swallowed, strengthened my resolve, and added, "I'm a Christian."

"Of course you're a Christian!" he bellowed. "Why else would you be standing here?"

I felt the color rise in my face. Armed soldiers flanked the magistrate. They were all staring at me, sniggering.

The magistrate spoke to the soldier on his right. "How can a creature be so blessed in body and so devoid of mind?" he cried.

"I prefer them dumb and shapely," the soldier replied.

The magistrate hauled himself out of his chair and approached me.

"As a favor to beauty," he announced to those assembled.

23

He grabbed my wrist and guided my hand to a bowl of incense.

"Take a pinch," he said.

I hesitated. His face reddened.

"Take a pinch!" he shouted.

I did.

Still holding my wrist, he moved it to the other side where there was a bowl of flame.

"Now drop the incense in the flames and swear your allegiance to the gods of Rome."

He held my hand over the flame.

I pulled it back and out of his grip. Then I dusted the incense from my fingers.

The magistrate was enraged. A torrent of unholy words flew in my face.

I didn't realize it at the time, but I had just witnessed an answer to my prayer for strength. Had I encountered a gentle magistrate who spoke in fatherly tones, I might have been persuaded to compromise my faith. But God was good in giving me this purple-faced, lecherous man who made it so easy to take a stand for holiness.

My sentence was swift in coming. It consisted of five words: "To the stews with her!"

I have to confess to you, I wasn't prepared for this. To die, yes. This was worse.

Soldiers grabbed me from both sides and dragged me through the streets. Stares, insults, spittle, and jeers accompanied me. The very people who earlier had smiled and waved at me were shouting and cursing and calling for my death.

They took me to the public baths and dumped me in a steamy room furnished with only a rough wooden bench. The door slammed behind me.

Overcome, I slumped onto the bench and wept. The dampness was suffocating, but not nearly as suffocating as the thoughts of what awaited me. There was only one reason for a woman to be at the public baths. My virginity was to be sacrificed to pagan lust.

I sat facing the door, cringing at the sounds of male laughter coming from the other side. Time and again footsteps approached and my heart would leap into my throat, only to hear them pass by. I worked myself into a panic over the expected sound of the door latch. By nightfall I was still alone and exhausted. Curling up in a corner, my face toward the door, I spent the night in fitful sleep.

At midmorning the latch sounded. I tensed.

A Roman soldier entered.

As he turned his back to latch the door I found myself eyeing his sword. Even if I managed to get it from him, what then? Would I use it? Could I plunge a blade into a man?

"Theodora."

The soldier spoke my name. Softly. How did he . . . ?

"Don't be afraid."

That's the way he said it. Just like an angel.

"Don't be afraid."

Not until he removed the helmet did I recognize him.

"Didymus!"

"We don't have much time."

"What are you doing in a soldier's uniform?"

"Take off your clothes."

"What? Shame! I will not!"

He wasn't listening. He was stripping off the uniform.

"Put this on," he said handing me the chest plate.

The truth of the situation began to dawn. Didymus was rescuing me. It was then that I saw how badly his hands were shaking.

"When you leave, keep your head down and don't speak to anyone. Make your way to the outskirts of the city. There's a group of believers waiting for you upstream near the outcropping of rock on the north side."

I was struck dumb. Didymus was sacrificing himself for me.

"Hurry!" he said.

My escape was surprisingly easy. I walked away from the stews unchallenged and quickly made my way upstream where I found a band of Christians exactly where Didymus said they would be.

The next day all of Antioch was abuzz about the Roman soldier who was second in line for my room at the baths and how he went to the stews expecting to find a virgin and found instead a young man dressed in women's clothing.

Didymus was hauled before the magistrate and condemned to death. That night I heard how Didymus learned of my plight and, against the advice of friends and family, concocted the rescue. I lay awake all night thinking about what he did for me.

By morning I was resolved to do the same for him. Slipping back into the city, I went to the tribunal to plead for the life of my friend.

My argument was simple. I was the guilty one. Didymus was acting out of the purest of motives. Certainly Rome would recognize and honor such loyalty. I begged the magistrate to release Didymus and return me to the stews. I vowed that this time I would remain there and willingly submit to the soldiers.

The magistrate listened to me without interruption. He sent for Didymus who was not pleased to see me, and I soon understood why. This magistrate knew nothing of honor or compassion. The familiar, taunting leer formed on his lips as he sentenced us both to death.

We were executed the next day.

But if you think our story sad, you miss its meaning! For in the twinkling of an eye, we were changed. Just as we shed our garments in the stews, at the moment of death we shrugged off our corruptible bodies and put on incorruptible ones.

As He always does, God worked everything for good. When the story of our mutual self-sacrifice was told, thousands of believers were strengthened in the faith. Some, like the twins who stood in line with their father, were young enough that they lived to see the day when the cross of Christ was lifted so high, it conquered the empire.

Dear friends, my encouragement to you is this: Do not fear the day of trial. Endure hardship, knowing that you will be stronger for it. Fear not those who can kill your body, for they can never take from you the life God has deposited within you. To Him be the glory.

In Christian love,
Theodora

P.S. My dear friend Didymus looks over my shoulder even as I write this. He sends his greetings.

# Homesick

### Jared

Loved ones,

Thinking back on the comment on perception I made in my first letter, I've attempted to resurrect some of the old feelings of what it was like to live on earth. They fade so quickly here. And as I thought about it, I began to realize how unnatural it felt, like wearing your shoes on the wrong feet.

I always thought of myself as a laid-back Californian, a guy who was satisfied with a good salary, a mortgage, a Mercedes, and *Monday Night Football*. Now, looking back on it all, I realize that running beneath the surface of my suburban Eden was a river of discontent. I didn't know it at the time, but I was homesick.

The signs of my homesickness were everywhere. There was a weariness that came from living in a world that equated friendship with a six-pack, that had to shoot up, drink down, or out-spend each other to feel good. It was tiresome listening to people who couldn't converse without expletives, cruel jokes, snide comments, and put-downs.

There was something inside of me that wouldn't let me buy into the world's values where profit was king and clothes were a substitute for self-confidence; where pride was worn like a necklace while spouses were treated like worn-out sneakers; where advertisements got louder as products got cheaper; and where a man's word was a bank check he couldn't cover.

You'd think that after centuries of history, people would have learned to get along. Yet even in my time the world remained a place where a lingering gaze could cause offense, position on the freeway could erupt in gunfire, and an errant word could launch a lawsuit. It was difficult to understand how people who could stand in line all night for concert tickets couldn't find time to visit their elderly relatives, or how they could know so much about a Hollywood entertainer and so little about their next-door neighbor.

The world scene made no sense. It seemed like the whole of humanity died a little every time a terrorist made a statement with a bomb, every time a father bruised the flesh of his child, and every time a world leader valued a piece of geography over the lives of those who lived on it.

I grew tired of living in a country that insisted you had to borrow from tomorrow to be happy today, where bankers practiced usury with a smile, where screen romance was always naked, and where everyone believed that life was about them.

I was homesick for a better world.

I didn't want to be angry anymore.

I hated that my days were spent balancing on a verbal tightrope so as not to offend anyone, and fending off fast-talking salesmen, political pollsters, credit card calls, and airport cults. There was something wrong about a world where a parent had to dread the ringing of the phone every time his child was late coming home; and where life expectancy was an equation based on the sum total of your weight, cholesterol, blood pressure, and triglycerides.

I longed to be accepted for who I was, not for my physical shape; to live in a world where people are known for their graces, not their blemishes; where joy is a person's first thought in the morning and peace his last thought at night; where people speak from the heart and where lies have been placed on the endangered species list, where words are bricks for bridges, not walls. I wanted to live in a world where awe is an everyday emotion.

The place I wanted to be was home. My soul longed to resonate with the universe, my heart to beat with the rhythm of the ocean waves, and my face to turn upward with the sunflowers in praise to God.

I wanted to live in a place where I could spend one eternity lost in my wife's embrace, and another rolling atop the grass with my kids. I wanted to laugh from the gut, cry unashamed with joy, be missed when I was gone, and march in step with an army of good men for some magnificent cause. I was tired of praying "on earth as it is in heaven." I wanted to live it now.

Looking back on it all, I never felt quite at home on earth. I'll take God's Kingdom any eternity. I can't imagine ever growing tired of sitting at Jesus' feet, or worshiping in God's throne room, or singing with the angelic host that appeared to the shepherds over the hills of Bethlehem.

But then, I guess if I were to grow tired of it, it wouldn't really be home.

Wishing you were here,
Jared

30

# My Greatest
# Spiritual Experience
## Shankala

Beloved,

Have you ever agreed to do something and afterwards wondered where your head was at the time? That's how I feel about writin' these letters. I wants to do them, mind you. It's just that now that the time has come, for the life of me I don't know what to say.

Besides that, I don't write pretty like the others. But Jared, bless his heart, says that that don't matter and I should just tell you what the Lord has done in my life. Sounds easy enough. I just loves praisin' my Lord.

So here goes.

In my life on earth my father was a powerful witch doctor. The whole province of Wallamo feared him. I grew up in a yard surrounded by a fence made of spears,

31

each spear coming from a man who died from one of my father's hexes or curses.

Father was an old man when I first heard missionaries teach about Jesus Christ. His body was used up, like a bar of soap after a hard day's wash. He was stooped over when he walked. Two servants was always at his side to help him up and down and to catch him when he stumbled.

The villagers said I was abandoning my father who had protected me with his magic all his life. They said that I brought an unfriendly demon into the hut that attacked him when he was weak. They were afraid. They believed the dark powers that had served my father would seek revenge on the whole village. My husband, Damato, was counted among them.

When the death wail sounded, thousands of people from all over the province came to mourn my father's death. Drums beat. Witch doctors danced up and down in front of the mourners, turning somersaults, tearin' their cheeks with long fingernails, poundin' their chests with fists. They used bundles of thorns to scratch their faces and arms and legs until blood flowed as a sign of their grief.

Many villagers were angry when I came to my father's funeral. They grew angrier when I refused to cut myself as was the custom.

One of the witch doctors danced wildly in front of me for a long time. The longer he danced, the angrier he became. Soon, everyone was watching. The witch doctor lunged at me, screaming curses. He would lunge, then back away, then lunge again, each time he grew bolder. Then, he began pokin' me with a stick, jabbin' my shoulders and chest. I did nothin'. Just stood there. In my mind I was praying to God, askin' Him to keep me strong and help me know what to do.

Suddenly, the drums stopped. The witch doctor came real close, within inches of me. He screamed in my face, shouting that my father's spirit cried out for vengeance. Then, he placed a curse on me, saying that before the comin' of the next day of Meskal—a sacrifice to the devil that was done every year—I would be dead. All the villagers near me shrank back, including some of the people from our church. That night my husband, Damato, took our son and ran away to another village.

I wish I could tell you that I was faithful and never doubted. But fear and anger were strong inside me. I was angry at Damato for stealing my son and leavin' me, and I was angry at God for letting him.

And I was afraid of what was goin' to happen to me. The dark powers are real. And powerful. I once watched a healthy man fall down dead at the instant my father said he would. Once my father covered a man with boils with a hex. Another man floated in air, and still another talked to my father with many different voices.

Even false witch doctors was dangerous. I had heard stories of how they assisted their hexes by placing poison in a person's food or water, or placing a poisonous snake in their hut at night. Their methods were many and effective.

The missionaries told me to put my faith in God. They were right, of course. And I did put my faith in God, as much as I was able to do at the time. But my fears lingered and grew stronger with the approaching of Meskal.

The curse attacked me where I was weakest. When I first became a believer, I'd wondered if I'd be strong enough to endure some great tragedy and still stay faithful. Sometimes I imagined such a tragedy—Damato dying, my son bein' killed in the field, or my eyes goin' dark, or a great illness coming upon me. When I saw others who experienced these things, I watched them and thought that if it were to happen to me, I could be strong. But now I was no longer certain. Then, I became ill.

Villagers clucked their tongues at me and said I should go to the witch doctor and beg him to save me. Church members came by daily to pray for me and bring me food that was safe to eat. But I feared it was too late. Had I already eaten something that had been poisoned? As the drums began beating to call the villagers to assemble for Meskal, the pain in my belly was unbearable.

It seems foolish now, but I was afraid to die. Even more, I was afraid that if I died, I would harm the work of Jesus among the Wallamo people. Everyone would believe I died from the witch doctor's curse.

On the day of Meskal, I was doubled over with pain. But I was alive. The witch doctor had said I would die before Meskal, and I didn't. God had answered my prayers.

I asked the missionaries to take me to the gathering so that everyone could see that Jesus was stronger than the devil. They told me I was too sick to travel, that they'd send a runner to tell everyone. But I knew some would not believe a runner. The only way they'd believe was if they saw me still alive at Meskal.

The sacrifice was held six miles from the village. I was taken there in a cart pulled by horses. We were barely a mile along the way when my pain became so great I thought for certain I was not goin' to make it. Unconsciousness fell upon me like a blanket. Each time it did, with God's strength, I managed to throw it off. But each time was more difficult than the last.

The sound of drums grew louder. As we drew closer we could see thousands upon thousands of people gathered for the sacrifice. Horsemen played games and threw spears at each other. The witch doctors danced and tumbled and cut themselves.

I was too weak to stand and had to be helped from the cart, but once standing I knew I had to walk on my own if I was to prove that Jesus was stronger than the devil. I prayed for Jesus to move my legs for me.

The drums fell silent when I stepped into the clearing. The crowd hushed. I saw my husband Damato and my son standing among the crowd. I tried to speak.

"You all knows me . . . "

My throat was dry, my voice weak. I had to begin again.

"You all knows me," I said. "My father was a great witch doctor. At his funeral a hex was put on me because of my faith in Jesus Christ. I was told I'd die before the next Meskal. But I'm not dead. Jesus has kept me alive. Jesus is more powerful than the witch doctors. And you'd be wise to leave this place and worship Jesus as I do."

Everyone looked at the witch doctor who'd cursed me. He stood there. Everyone saw he had no power over me.

I had nothin' more to say, so I walked back to the cart and was taken back to my hut in the village.

In the weeks that followed, I kept on praying for my people and my healing. We'd witnessed a great victory. But still, I was sick. Nights were the worst. Not only was the pain strongest at night, but so was my fear of dying.

Then, one morning at dawn, I felt no pain and I knew I was healed. Jesus had answered my prayer.

That was the day I awoke in heaven.

I don't knows why I was surprised. After all, isn't that just like Jesus—He took the thing I feared most and turned it into the greatest experience of my life.

My battle with pain is over. News of my faith and my death has saved many of the villagers from the wickedness of the witch doctors, including Damato and my son.

If I have a word of encouragement for you it is this—Beloved, fear not the test. For King Jesus will give you the strength for the test and will deliver you with a surprising joy. He'll take the thing you fear most and make it your greatest victory.

Still amazed,
Shankala

# If We Had to Do It All Over Again

*Lessons We Learned in Life*

# The Day Anger Died
## Theodora

Beloved,

A band of Scythians killed my father when I was fifteen years old. It was a needless slaughter.

He was no threat to them. A cloth merchant, he was returning from Iconium with a small caravan of traders when the Scythians attacked without provocation. That's their way.

My father was a good man. A good father. A deacon in the church. An honest businessman. It was beyond understanding why God would let such a godly man die at the hands of such godless people.

The Scythians were notorious, tattooed marauders who swept down on innocent villages and caravans with dust and thunder. They lived on horseback and worshiped the spears and battle-axes and bows with which they killed. The howling that preceded their attacks struck fear in the stoutest of hearts.

There wasn't anything good about them. Their women were warriors, as well as the men. Barbarous even to barbarians, they offered human sacrifices, scalped and flayed their slain enemies, drank the blood of their victims, then used the skulls for drinking cups. War was their business and their pleasure.

How could God allow such animals to take my father from me? When I heard the news, there was not enough comfort in the world to console me.

For years my anger cast a black shadow over everything in my life. I loathed it yet lived with it. I was angry at everyone and everything—angry at God for not protecting my father; angry at my mother because after a time she stopped being angry; angry at members of my church because they said I should forgive the men who killed my father. What did they know of my pain? And I was angry at myself for being angry. I didn't like myself when I was angry. (Even now the remembrance of my anger brings discomfort to me, but it is for your good that I recall it.)

A few weeks after my father's death our bishop preached a message. He began by saying the message was about the all-encompassing Christ, but when he read the selected text I became suspicious that he chose it with me in mind. That too made me angry.

He read from a copy of the Apostle Paul's letter to the church at Colossae (Col. 3:8–13):

> But now ye also put off all these: anger, wrath, malice, blasphemy, filthy communication out of your mouth . . .

Five things were listed. I heard only one. Anger.

As I was accustomed to doing, I shut myself off to what followed. This time, however, God's Spirit breached the barrier and the flow of words continued unchecked.

> . . . put off the old man with his deeds; And have put on the new *man*, which is renewed in knowledge after the image of him that created him: Where there is neither Greek nor Jew, circumcision nor uncircumcision, Barbarian, Scythian . . .

Scythian!

The word pierced me. My anger flared.

I glanced up expecting to challenge the bishop's gaze with my own. Surely he'd added that word as a direct attack on me. But all I saw was his head bowed in concentration as he continued reading the text.

> . . . but Christ is all, and in all. Put on therefore, as the elect of God, holy and beloved, bowels of mercies, kindness, humbleness of mind, meekness, longsuffering; Forbearing one another, and forgiving one another, if any man have a quarrel against any: even as Christ forgave you, so also *do* ye.

Mercy. Kindness. Longsuffering. Forgiving.

No. I refused. It was asking too much of me to forgive the heathen barbarian who murdered my father.

I wish I could tell you that the bishop's message weighed on my heart that week—it did—and that I soon learned the healing power of forgiveness, but I can't, because it didn't happen that way. My anger grew even more. I wanted revenge, not mercy.

I was convinced the apostle didn't know what he was asking me to do. He didn't know the Scythians like I knew them. They didn't deserve forgiveness. They were a race of savages. There was nothing worth redeeming in them.

And so I lived with my anger. Every morning as I dressed, I put it on as a cloak around my shoulders. It was a heavy burden, but I was proud to bear it, for it served as a memorial to my father and gave testimony to the injustice that struck him down.

Imagine my surprise the day I came home to God's eternal kingdom. My father was there to greet me, as I knew he would be. Standing beside him was the Scythian who slew him.

Father embraced me. Then he put his hands on my shoulders and said, "Let it go, Theodora. There is no place for your anger here."

I looked at the Scythian, the object of my hatred, and said, "No, Father. I cannot do what you ask."

(I still can't believe I said that. But by that time I was so accustomed to my anger I couldn't imagine living without it. It had become part of me. Besides, didn't he know that I wore it for him?)

Disappointment filled my father's eyes. My heart sank at the sight.

"But you don't understand!" I cried.

"No, Theodora," he replied, "it is you who don't understand."

The Scythian stepped forward to speak. I recoiled. There was nothing he had to say that I wanted to hear. He spoke anyway. His manner was gentle, his voice tender, not at all what I'd expected. He said, "Theodora, it is because of your father that I'm here."

I looked away. In truth, I didn't want him here.

The Scythian continued. "I don't deserve to be here," he said, "not with godly men like your father."

At this my father fidgeted. The Scythian didn't seem to notice. His gaze, his posture, his every movement was focused on me as though he'd been preparing for this moment for a lifetime.

"I looked into the eyes of every man I killed," he said, "and saw the fear, the hatred . . . the same hatred that I see in your eyes even now."

I felt shame but shrugged it off. There was nothing this man could say that would make me forgive him for what he did to me.

"Your father was different," he said. "Even as he lay mortally wounded, I saw no fear, no hatred in his eyes. He looked at me and said, 'I forgive you just as Jesus Christ forgave me.'"

The Scythian fell silent, for we both knew what he had done next. He killed my father.

"But I couldn't kill his words," he said. "From that day they hounded me. I couldn't flee them and I couldn't fight them. Every day the force of their blows grew stronger until finally they brought me to my knees. Your father proved to be the superior warrior, for he bested me with his forgiveness."

The Scythian sank to his knees.

"You want to slay me," he said. "I can see it in your eyes." He paused. Then said, "Go ahead. As Jesus Christ and your father forgave me, so I forgive you."

*Forgive me?*

My anger flared. But it was a dying gasp. For at that moment I realized there was only one barbarian here. It was me. And using the same weapon with which my father bested him, the Scythian bested me.

It was on that day my anger died.

Since then I've heard many stories of how the Scythian and my father watched over me all my earthly years. Some said they've never known two men to be so united in a cause. I have two fathers now.

Beloved, don't make the same mistake I made. Don't be proud of your anger. Don't think you're justified. It's a heavy burden you don't have to carry. Trust in God and let it go, for He can bring good out of the greatest injustice.

There is healing power in forgiveness. Learn it now, or learn it later. But you will learn it. It's a Kingdom trait.

Angry no more,
Theodora

# The Benefits of Stress
### Dr. Everett Parker

Beloved,

It amuses me that every generation thinks it is subject to greater stress than those who lived before them. Nobody knows the troubles we've seen, or so the saying goes; and compared to modern day pressures, "the good ole days" were peaceful and serene.

Nonsense.

Imagine the anxiety of a woman who makes a mistake in judgment and it costs her family their home, their livelihood, and their security.

This was Eve in the Garden of Eden.

Imagine the anxiety of parents as they stand over the broken body of their firstborn son, the victim of a brutal slaying, knowing that their other son is the murderer.

Again Eve, this time with her husband Adam, and sons Abel and Cain.

Stress is a fact of life. It has been since Eden. However, that doesn't stop every generation from doing studies that reveal "shocking new evidence" that reveals there is a worldwide epidemic of stress. Believe me, wherever two or more are gathered, there stress will be.

Another common fallacy is to categorize stress as a disease. It isn't. By labeling stress a disease we think that, with proper precautions, we can avoid it. We can't. And if it's a disease, that makes us victims. We aren't. So we spend a great deal of time, money, and effort developing theories and lessons on how to avoid stress, thereby failing to benefit from it.

You read that correctly. Stress has benefits.

Most Christians aren't any better than the rest of the world when it comes to appreciating the benefits of stress. Think about it. What is the normal advice we offer to those under stress? Pray. Trust God. Be patient. This too shall pass. Not bad advice in most circumstances. But what do you do when you pray to God, saying, "Lord, I'm under a lot of stress right now." And He replies, "I know. I'm causing it."

Does that surprise you? The fact is, God is one of the leading causes of stress.

I know that's not what you want to hear, but it's true. Stress is one of the benefits of being God's chosen people.

Like most people, I bucked when it came to learning this lesson. How well I remember the night God taught it to me. I'd been called away from the army hospital to deliver a baby in town. It seemed the whole town was anxiously awaiting this birth. Nell was a precious woman, loved by all. I'd delivered her twenty years earlier, and now I was going to deliver her firstborn.

It was a troubled pregnancy from the start, and I had done my best to prepare the family for a difficult birth.

46

Nell was optimistic. Such was her nature. Everyone was infected by it. You have to remember that in those days death was a staple of life. The war was on. I mean the *war* was on. We were tired of it. Every birth was a symbol of hope for the future.

That made the death of Nell's baby that much harder for us to accept. I did my best to save her, but it just wasn't good enough. Truth be told, I was fortunate I didn't lose the mother as well.

As you might suspect, Nell took it hard. She was the oldest of eleven children and so it fell upon her to help raise her brothers and sisters. It was hard for any of us to imagine her without a little one perched on her hip, or her holding a hand, or having a whole line of them straggling after her.

And Nell was never one to complain. Children weren't a chore to her. All this made the death of her own child that much harder to understand.

If things weren't bad enough, the complications of the birth were such that Nell would never be able to get pregnant again. It seemed as though that girl's sole reason for existence had been taken from her. For if ever there was a woman created to be a mother, it was Nell.

Never have I felt so helpless in a situation. I offered a few feeble words of reassurance and returned to the hospital. All in all, it had been one hellish day. Five amputations. Seven deaths. A dozen new cases of typhoid. A fifteen-year-old boy who lost his sight when his rifle exploded in his face. And then, this—the death of Nell's child. I was tired and angry.

My wife and I made a vow at the beginning of our marriage that we would never go to bed angry with each other, this in keeping with the Scriptures. When she died, I suffered a dark spell of depression. After that I

47

made a similar vow to God, that I would never go to bed angry with Him. The night Nell's baby died I didn't go to bed. Instead, I opened my Bible. We had to talk.

As He is so capable of doing, God spoke clearly to my heart. Only it was a lesson I didn't want to learn. My eyes fell upon the passage that relates the incident of Jeremiah and the potter. What got my attention was the phrase "as the clay is in the potter's hand, so are ye in mine hand."

I was familiar with the image. God is the potter, we are the clay. But why had God chosen this image tonight? He could have said, I am the King, you are the subjects; or as in other places, I am the Shepherd, you are the sheep. Why the potter?

I pondered the passage. The clay was passive to the potter's efforts to remove its impurities, then fashion it according to His good pleasure. Was that the lesson I needed to learn? That God was sovereign in all things and we shouldn't question that?

There had to be more.

Then I considered how a potter selects the clay and shapes it with a purpose in mind. Even so, God has a purpose for each of us. That too, I could accept. But still there had to be more.

I decided to locate other Scripture passages where this Hebrew word for potter was used. What I found was both revealing and alarming. The same word used in other passages was not translated *potter* at all.

Judges 2:15: *The Lord was angry against Israel,* . . . *"and they were greatly* distressed."

Judges 10:9: *The Ammonites crossed the Jordan to attack Israel, "so that Israel was sore* distressed."

1 Samuel 30:6: *David's men threatened to stone him, "and David was greatly* distressed."

I remember sitting back in my chair as the truth worked in me. The word for potter is the noun form of the verb distress. That means a potter is a craftsman who works his will by distressing the clay with a specific purpose in mind.

*As the clay is in the potter's hand, so are ye in mine hand.*

That was the lesson! God, the potter, distresses us, the clay, so that we might become fit vessels for His use.

I thought of the many raw army recruits that had passed through Cairo, Illinois, over the years. They too were stressed by superior officers for a purpose, to prepare them for battle. While their stress was unpleasant at the time, the goal was not their discomfort but their survival. So it is with God and us. The stress we endure is His way of preparing us for His work.

I closed my Bible, satisfied that I had learned the lesson God wanted me to learn that night.

But He wasn't finished with me.

My thoughts returned to the vessel in the potter's hands. Molded, shaped, but still not ready for service. It was still wet, pliable. The potter wasn't finished.

My heart felt heavy when I realized the truth. After the stress comes the fire.

Suddenly, some troubling passages of Scripture took on new meaning.

1 Peter 4:12: *Beloved, think it not strange concerning the fiery trial which is to try you, as though some strange thing happened unto you.*

James 1:2–4: *My brethren, count it all joy when ye fall into divers temptations; Knowing this, that the trying of your faith worketh patience. But let patience have her perfect work, that ye may be perfect and entire, wanting nothing.*

Romans 5:3–4: *Not only so, but we also rejoice in our sufferings, because we know that suffering produces perseverance; perseverance, character; and character, hope.*

It was a painful lesson, but necessary. God uses stress to make us something we cannot be by ourselves, to give us purpose and greater value. Stress benefits us. Without stress, there is no salvation. Neither can there be service without strain, wisdom without study, or maturity without adversity.

Months later God confirmed this lesson. And He did it with Nell.

Once again I was called to town to care for a woman in our church who was close to giving birth. It was another troubled pregnancy. While I had learned to trust God in these things, I still felt inadequate as I approached the house.

When I entered the house, there was Nell, sitting with the woman on the sofa, holding her hands, and saying, "I know exactly how you feel."

She was God's vessel for this moment, molded, shaped, and fresh from the fire. A priceless work of the Master Potter.

One of His vessels,
Everett Parker, M.D.

# If I Knew Then
# What I Know Now
## Shankala

Beloved,

I wouldn't go so far as to say there are regrets in heaven. Neither is there shame. But there are times when you looks back on your earthly life and says to yourself, "Shame! You knows better than that!"

The only 'scuse you can give is that you just weren't seein' things clearly at the time. Like Jared said, it's a matter of perspective. On earth, you sees things pretty much like you would walking through a deep canyon. You knows where you been, and you can sees a little ways ahead, but only as far as the next turn and then you has no idea what's beyond that. While here in heaven, we sees things from the mountaintop. From here, a person can see nigh on to forever.

And another thing about that canyon view on earth, it's just as King David sang—that you never knows when something's going to jump out at you from the shadows. Life's like that, especially not knowin'. But from the mountaintop all the doubts and fears of the canyon look foolish because you can sees so much more at a glance.

I guess that's what I wants to talk to you about in this letter 'cause we've all been in the canyon where you are now and, unlike you, we've also been to the mountaintop. If I had to do it all over again I wouldn't have wasted my earthly breath like I did telling the God of the mountaintop the lay of the land in the canyon as I seen it.

Sounds sort of silly when it's put that way, don't it? But let me tell you, life is full of so-called experts who's always leadin' other people to believe that they can see things more clearly than God. Like a blind man telling other blind men what a rainbow looks like.

So if I had to do it all over again, I'd take God at His word, without question, and that would be that. I'd live for certain knowin' God's ways is always best. No doubts. No arguments. No exceptions.

And I wouldn't be so uppity as to insist on having to understand everything either.

Now don't you raise your eyebrows at me like that. You knows you do it too. It's not like we say to His face, "God, I heard what You said, but I just don't believe it." No, instead, we say, "O Lord, all I wants is to understand. If I understand what You wanted me to do, Lord believe me, I'd do it! I just wants to understand."

Shame on us for sayin' such things.

First of all, God don't need to explain nothin' to us. He's God and we're His creatures, and we're better off when we don't get the two confused.

Besides, why do you think you need things explained to you anyway? Does the stone ask the builder to explain why it's being placed in the wall where he lays it? What do stones know of foundations and walls and archways? And what do canyon-dwellers know about the view from the mountaintop?

God is nobody's fool. He knows all that question-asking is nothin' more than an excuse to put off doing what you know you should be doin'. Let me tell you this: Either you trusts Him or you don't. No amount of explaining is going to change that.

And askin' for a sign isn't much better.

I remembers hearing a sermon preached once on Hezekiah. It was the story where King Hezekiah was ill and God sent him the great prophet Isaiah to tell him that he wasn't going to die. Now the king needed to hear this message because he was weepin' something fierce.

So to prove to the king that he would be granted fifteen more years of life, God gave him a sign. God said that the shadow on the stone stairway that was built by Ahaz would move backwards ten steps. Now this was a powerful sign, and it was given to him to prove that what the prophet Isaiah was saying to him was true.

I remember how happy hearing that sermon made me. I liked having a sign-givin' God like that. I knew I would sleeps easier at night just thinking about those signs as I drifted off.

And so that week I prayed and asked God to give me signs that would prove to me that my prayers would be answered, just like He did for King Hezekiah.

I prayed that my crops would be plentiful that year. For a sign, I asked God to make it rain the next morning so that I would know that my crops would be plentiful. Then I prayed that my cow would birth a calf in the spring. For a sign, I asked God to make my cow low three times at sunset for three nights in a row. And then I prayed for good health because all that winter I had suffered a terrible cough. For a sign, I asked God to speak to our missionary and tell him to come to my house with a message that God promised to bless me with health for the coming year.

And then I waited, knowin' that signs would come because they were easy ones, nothin' so hard as making a shadow go backwards ten steps.

Well, Monday morning came and I awoke and listened for the sound of rain on the roof of my hut. But there was no rain. In fact, the day was sunny and hotter than the day before. My heart melted with the heat. Then, things got worse.

That night my cow didn't low at sunset, and the missionary didn't come. So I gave God a couple extra days, thinking He might be extra busy with doin' signs for other folks. I waited a week, then two weeks, but the signs never came.

Without the signs, I believed the worst would happen. My crops were going to fail, my cow wouldn't birth a calf, and I'd be sick come winter. I was miserable and wished I'd never asked for the signs. Knowin' that bad things was goin' to happen was worse than not knowin'.

A few Sundays later as I was leaving the worship service, our missionary asked me if something was troubling me. He said my eyes were downcast and my spirit was so low it was dragging in the dirt.

I feared telling him about all the bad things that was goin' to happen to me. And a part of me feared telling him about the signs. I guess I was ashamed that God did not see fit to answer my prayers the way I wanted Him to.

But the missionary kept askin' me, so finally I told him about my three prayers and the three signs. He smiled.

That smile of his didn't make me feel any better. All-of-a-sudden-like I felt like a child who should have know'd better.

The missionary said, "How many signs do you need, Shankala?"

His question surprised me. I only asked for three. "Did I ask for too many?"

His smile grew wider. "It's just that God has already given you so many signs," he said.

Well that knocked me off my stoop. I couldn't imagine getting a sign from God and not knowin' about it.

The missionary said, "God has given us so many signs! He gave us the sign of the manger to remind us that He is always with us. He gave us the sign of the cross to remind us that Jesus died for our sins. He gave us the sign of the empty tomb to remind us that death has no hold on us. He has given us the sign of baptism to remind us that just as Jesus was resurrected, so we will be raised. And He gave us the sign of His Holy Spirit, like a seal stamped on our hearts, as a guarantee that we are indeed heirs of the Kingdom."

I don't have to tell you I was mighty humbled. All the while I was asking for signs, I didn't even appreciate the ones God had given me.

Oh, there's one more thing I needs to tell you before I close this letter. You remember the things I prayed for? God answered them. Every one. My crops came in bountifully, my cow birthed a calf, and I went all winter without catching a cough. God was good to me even though I had so much to learn about His ways.

So, if I had to do it all over again, you knows what I'd do? I'd walk that narrow canyon of life again, but this time I'd trust the God of the mountaintop, knowin' that there was nothin' in that canyon up ahead that He couldn't already see and take care of for me.

Living atop the mountain,<br>
Shankala

# The Land of Mirages
## Jared

Loved ones,

Life on earth can be described as a trek through a land that is riddled with one mirage after another. For centuries these deceptive visions have been the ruin of many.

A mirage promises something it can't deliver. Water to a thirsty man, to take the most common example. Thus, the very nature of a mirage is to deceive and to do it in a most cruel way, because a mirage plays on our desires. The word mirage shares the same root as the word mirror. In other words, a mirage reflects our own desire back at us. If we didn't desire to be prosperous, why then would we envy the wicked when they prosper?

The psalmist did.

*My feet were almost gone; my steps had well nigh slipped. For I was envious at the foolish, when I saw the prosperity of the wicked* (Ps. 73:2–3).

Take a look at the words he used to describe them—proud, ill-tempered, gluttons, full of malice, boastful, and arrogant. Who in their right mind would want to be like them? Nobody. Ah, but then, who wants to have what they have? We all do. And the mirage takes shape.

"See how the gods favor the sacrilegious," said the ancient.

So why do I try to do the right thing? Why am I considerate of others? Why am I honest, if it's every man for himself? Why am I considerate, if nice guys finish last? Don't we live in a competitive society? If I don't speak out for myself, who will?

I remember reading of an elaborate funeral in Oakland, California. The man who had died earned as much as $400,000 a month. People lined the street to see his casket as it traveled an eight-mile route through the city in a horse-drawn hearse followed by a procession of Rolls Royce cars. Tuxedoed ushers assisted the mourners. The deceased was known for his wealthy lifestyle. Big houses. Wanting for nothing.

The funeral of a king? A movie star? An athlete? No, the man in the ornate bronze casket was a drug kingpin who made a living supplying cocaine to thousands of addicts.

In the words of the psalmist:

> Therefore pride is their necklace;
>     they clothe themselves with violence.
> From their callous hearts comes iniquity;
>     the evil conceits of their minds
>         know no limits.
> They scoff, and speak with malice;
>     in their arrogance they threaten
>         oppression.
> Their mouths lay claim to heaven,

and their tongues take possession of
    the earth.
Therefore their people turn to them
    and drink up waters in abundance.
They say, "How can God know?
    Does the Most High have
    knowledge?"
This is what the wicked are like—
    always carefree, they increase in
    wealth.
Surely in vain have I kept my heart
    pure;
    in vain have I washed my hands in
    innocence.

Psalm 73:6–13

I remember thinking the same thing. Why am I knocking myself out trying to do right and be fair, which barely earns me a living, while this man scoffs at everything holy and lives like a king?

Ever feel that way?

If you do, you're believing in a mirage.

While the casket of the drug kingpin was paraded around the streets of Oakland, the man was standing before the Almighty God giving an account for his actions. That's the real story behind the mirage.

Again, from the psalmist: *But as for me, my feet had almost slipped; I had nearly lost my foothold. For I envied the arrogant when I saw the prosperity of the wicked* (Ps. 73:2–3).

My feet almost slipped. Almost. I nearly lost my foothold. Nearly. The mirage looked so real, I almost believed it to be real. Almost.

Too many people are fooled by the mirage. They do things they know they shouldn't do. And then, for them, it's too late. Such as Zeek, a man who believed the mirage.

For Zeek the mirage was having a million dollars, living tax-free on a cozy little Caribbean island where the sun was warm and living was easy. His dream was to escape his daily obligations and the drudgery of work and to live in the company of his two favorite dogs and an attractive young girlfriend to help him spend his money.

His dream came true. When interviewed by a reporter, Zeek was living on Grenada in the West Indies. His notoriety came shortly after pulling off one of the greatest cons in the history of American horse racing. A con that netted him $1.3 million.

Zeek was not a professional con man. He was a trainer of thoroughbred horses. One of the best in the business. He was also a gambler whose checks would bounce from time to time, but the bankers soon learned that Zeek always made the checks good. In return for their patience, Zeek wined and dined his bankers and treated them to more than a few winning bets at the tracks. So when Zeek would ask them to hold a check or two until he could cover them, it seemed the business thing to do.

That's when the mirage began to form. When Zeek took note of how easy it was to be trusted at the banks and the track, he saw his dreams shimmering in the distance. He made his play.

Sixty-one checks later Zeek, his two favorite dogs, and a girlfriend were winging their way to Grenada, a Caribbean island with no extradition treaty with the United States. He left behind a wife, three children, and a host of red-faced bankers.

Zeek has it all. Money. Plenty of sun. He owns a yacht. The fishing's great. He doesn't have to work or worry about checks bouncing. There's only one problem. A mirage promises something it cannot deliver.

Zeek wants to come home.

I know exactly how Zeek feels. I never ran a con game, but I chased several mirages in my life only to wind up just as dissatisfied. In my day, advertising agencies and Hollywood spent millions of dollars a year creating mirages—the correct hair color, clothing, breath odor, the whiteness of your teeth, and tan skin, all of which will attract friends. That's the mirage. Only it can't deliver what it promises because the people these things attract know little about what it means to be a friend.

Romance and love are one and the same thing. Another mirage. There is a depth of love that puts romance to shame. Unfortunately, too many couples know only the shallow romance waters and never wade into a deeper relationship where satisfaction lies.

What's the lesson I learned that I want to pass along to you? Only this: There are no mirages in God's Word. There are no mirages in God's Kingdom. When you follow God's ways, you never have to wonder whether or not the image will fade and you'll be left with disappointing reality. God's ways are reality.

Don't be fooled. If, like the psalmist, your feet are almost slipping and you're beginning to believe that the wicked prosper, and that lasting happiness and contentment is found in the accumulation of things, run—don't walk—to the nearest quiet place where you can pray. Ask God to show you the truth. Ask Him to make plain to you the future of the godless. And when you see things from the viewpoint of God's Kingdom, the mirage will dissipate.

It always does.

> One who exchanged the good life for the God-life,
> Jared

# 10

# Teraphim
### Dr. Everett Parker

Beloved,

You're not fooling anyone. You may think you are, but the only person you're fooling is yourself. It's time you take stock of yourself.

One of the things I learned in my lifetime is that people often think of themselves more highly than do their neighbors. There's a reason for this. We have a tendency to *deceive [our] own selves* (James 1:22).

It's a common practice. On more than one occasion the people of Israel were called on it. *Now therefore put away, said [Joshua], the strange gods which are among you, and incline your heart unto the LORD God of Israel* (Josh. 24:23).

It's not that they weren't worshiping God; they were. They were lifting their hands in praise. They were making the appropriate sacrifices. They were giving their offerings. They would stand and listen as the Word of

God was read to them. They listened to the teachings of the priests. They recited daily the Shema—*Hear, O Israel: The* LORD *our God is one* LORD*: And thou shalt love the* LORD *thy God with all thine heart, and with all thy soul, and with all thy might* (Deut. 6:4–5).

However, at the same time they were fingering the little household gods called teraphim they carried in their pockets or placed on shelves in their houses. While claiming to be the people of the all-knowing, all-wise God of Abraham, Isaac, and Jacob, they needed a god that was a little more visible and touchable. They were fooling themselves about their allegiance to God.

However, they should be given credit for one thing. They were more open about their divided loyalties than we are. And while we think we're better at hiding the little gods that we worship, we're only deceiving ourselves. It's as plain to those who know us as if we shaped them in clay and set them on our mantels.

You think they don't know you're not as dedicated to God as you say you are? The shape of modern teraphim are in the choices you make, the time you spend, the things for which you're willing to sacrifice, and the level of your emotions. When Joshua confronted the people of Israel, he said, *"You are witnesses against yourselves"* (Josh. 24:22). Truer words were never spoken.

A person's real values are determined not by what he says he values, but by his actions. There are four ways to test yourself to reveal your true values. Are you bold enough to take the test?

*Choices*. Your choices are a visible demonstration of your values. The places you choose to go. The activities in which you choose to participate. The places and activities in which you choose *not* to participate. Given the choice, what you do reveals the things that are of value to you.

*Time.* The priorities of your time indicate your values. Your use of recreational time and discretionary time reveal what is foremost in your heart.

*Sacrifice.* What things are you willing to sacrifice for? Stay later than expected? Give up something you value for a cause of greater value? This goes beyond convenience. What are the things you're willing to do even when it costs you something?

*Emotions.* What are the things in life that give you great satisfaction when you do them and cause you personal grief when you're unable to do them? What are the things you feel guilty about when you do them, or don't do them? What things can you do that never cause you guilt? These too can reveal your true values.

When your choices, time, sacrifice, and emotions don't verify what you say you believe, they become as visible to others as the teraphim were to the neighbors of the Israelites.

Joshua was right when he pointed out to the people of Israel that they stood at a crossroads. It was time for them to make it clear to everyone whether or not they were followers of God. It was time for them to put away their little household gods and serve the true God with a sincere heart.

And so it is with you. You stand at the crossroads. And no one can choose for you which way you will go. You have to choose for yourself. It's time to put away the things that do not bring honor to God. It's time to stop fooling yourself, because you're not fooling anyone else. You are a witness against yourself.

The time for indecision is past.

I read in the newspaper a story that President Abraham Lincoln told. (He was forever telling stories like these, sometimes much to the chagrin of his Cabinet and generals.) Anyway, this story was about a blacksmith who heated a piece of iron in the forge, not knowing what he would make out of it. His first thought was to make a horseshoe, but he changed his mind. Then he thought he'd make something else out of it. After hammering awhile, he changed his mind again and started fashioning something else altogether. By this time he'd so hammered the iron that it was not good for much of anything. Holding it up with his tongs, he looked at it in disgust. He thrust the piece of iron into a tub of water and watched it hiss. "Well, at least I made a fizzle out of it!" he exclaimed.

Such is a life of indecision—little more than a fizzle.

In Joshua's words, *"Choose you this day whom ye will serve"* (Josh. 24:15).

As part of the cloud of witnesses, I have often been encouraged to witness the choices God's people have made. So it was with great interest that I followed the early career of Samuel Parkes Cadman. The son of an English businessman, Cadman surrendered to the call of God in his life at the age of sixteen. He resolved to become a Christian minister. In time he passed the college entrance exams and began his formal training. Before finishing college, he married Lillian Wooding, a devout young Christian. They had three children.

In 1890 Cadman left England and sailed for America. Leaving his wife behind, he searched for a place where he could establish himself in the ministry and build a home so he could send for his family. He was given a preaching appointment in New York with a salary of only $600 a year. The church didn't have a parsonage, so Cadman had to build one almost single-handedly.

With such a small income, he was soon in debt and his attempt to save enough money to bring his wife to America was increasingly futile. Then, a successful New York lawyer, upon hearing Cadman preach, offered him $10,000 to join his law firm. Cadman replied that he wasn't a lawyer. So the man increased his offer to $20,000 just for him to plead cases; he insisted all he wanted was Cadman's eloquence.

Cadman again refused, saying he was a minister, not a lawyer. The man upped the offer to $25,000. It would take the minister more than forty years to make this amount of money. Here was the answer to Cadman's dream of bringing his wife to America.

Cadman looked the lawyer in the eye. He said, "You have made a mistake. It's not a question of money. I'm a minister. I shall always be a minister."

Let me tell you, the cloud cheered when they heard that. Here was a man with no teraphim in his pockets.

I must draw this letter to its conclusion. It's time for you to choose. Will you put away the little gods that distract you from serving the One, True God? Or will you go on deceiving yourself? The choice is yours.

Standing with Joshua,
Everett Parker, M.D.

# Squash Faith
### Shankala

Beloved,
I know how to grow squash. Probably the best thing that ever did grow in my garden was squash. Maybe 'cause it didn't take much to grow a squash. Plant the seed. Water it a little. The vine came and after that the squash. Didn't take much work, didn't take much water, but then no one ever came to my door asking to see my squash either.

Not like them redwoods in California. Never even heard of them until after I passed through the veil, but ooooeeee! If you wants to talk about something growin', we gots to talk about them redwoods. Three hundred feet and more! Now that'll get someone's attention. Not like my squash.

Now if I could grow a three-hundred-foot squash, maybe people would travel to see it like they do them redwoods, maybe not. A three-hundred-foot green and yellow squash with warts the size of a goat don't exactly inspire a person, does it? But then, I'm beginning to wander down the wrong path with this letter with a thought like that.

The lesson I wants to talk about in this letter is the difference between my squash and them grand redwoods in California. Not their size, mind you, but the time it takes to grow them.

When God wants to grow a squash, He takes a couple of months. When He wants to grow a redwood, He takes hundreds of years. The end result is worth noting.

So when God wants to grow a believer, He's going to take His good sweet time because you're worth more to Him than a squash or a redwood. And when He wants to grow a Kingdom, He takes even longer.

I say this to you because it seems everyone nowadays is in a hurry. They wants to grow up fast. They wants to live the fruit of the Spirit within days of their salvation, and preach like Paul within weeks.

Nonsense.

Growth takes time and God's in no hurry.

The temptation is to hurry things along. Christian leaders want to defeat evil within their lifetime. But that won't happen. Evil will continue until our Jesus returns and wraps time up in a bundle and tosses that monster Lucifer in the pit. So when you battle evil, it's best to think in terms of redwood, not squash.

For instance, in Theodora's day when Christians were hunted down and killed for sport, they didn't gain the victory over Rome in one generation, or even one century. But Christianity did indeed prevail in redwood years.

And in my day, the evil Mr. Hitler was pushing his way all around Europe like an infant throwing a tantrum.

Those were sad days indeed. He called his way the lightning strike and promised it would last for a thousand years. It hit hard, but it didn't last but a handful of years. He might have called it lightning, but it was a squash effort. Christianity survived Hitler too. It's still standing, like the redwood.

You have to remember, you're part of a marathon race, not a sprint. There are other runners from other generations that have gone before you; others will come after you. What makes you think your run is any more important than their run? We're all part of the same race. Each of us runs the race the best we can and Father will give us the victory. Over all evil, for all time. So run hard, run steady, run faithful, always remembering it's a long race.

And then when you think 'bout your own growth, think redwood, not squash. Everyone wants to grow up so fast nowadays and do things they're not ready for. Christians who have been saved for just a few months or years want to preach! Imagine that! What can a one-year-old teach anyone about how to live their lives? It just doesn't make sense.

Read the Word God has given you. What does it say about teachers? They're not called elders for nothin'. And to have preachers who take someone else's life insights and parade them around on a stage as their own, well that's fraud. Let a man study God's Word for himself and sit alone in his prayer chamber listening to the Holy Spirit, and speak from a full heart and a worthy life. Don't get me wrong, we can all learn something from the saints who have gone before us, and we should. But there's a difference between parroting someone else's words and speaking from a life-changing experience.

We need redwood growth in our preachers, not squash.

Well, I guess I've done had my say for now. If I were to boil this mess of pottage down to a few words, I guess I'd remind you that growth takes time. Every day is a classroom in which you learn how to be a disciple if you keep your eyes open and listen. The Spirit will help you understand.

Brothers and sisters, this message comes from my heart. Your best is my heart's desire.

Living among the redwoods of faith,<br>
Shankala

# The Tears of Paul

**Theodora**

Beloved,

The story I'm about to tell you is a sad story. It's a story of deceit and betrayal, of a relationship battered, abused, and broken. It's the stuff tears are made of.

Persis and Cyril were lovers. They were created for each other, at least that's what everyone thought. All of Antioch seemed to delight in their romance. As their impending wedding drew nearer, news of it became standard fare in the marketplace, along with the weather and prices. And when the day of the wedding arrived, so many businesses shut down it was like a holiday.

Just the way Persis and Cyril looked at each other, the way they touched each other's hands, their smiles, these and a hundred other little demonstrations reminded us what it was like to be in love. It was joyous.

It hadn't always been that way. When Cyril was younger he was a scoundrel and a roughneck, and when he began courting Persis more than one concerned friend warned her that he was no good. But the love of a woman can sometimes work magic on a man, and in the case of Cyril the change was no less than a miracle.

After a time it was impossible to think of one without thinking of the other. In the eyes of all Antioch, the two had indeed become one flesh.

It didn't last.

After only two months of marriage, Cyril's eye began to wander. He was seen with women other than his wife. He began frequenting all the places he'd been known to frequent before he met Persis. One night he didn't come home. Then another. After that he was gone for days without so much as a word to Persis.

Meanwhile, Persis waited for him, never knowing when he might return home. And when he did come home, he was drunk and argumentative and combative. Lovers had become enemies. And the town that once shared their love grieved over what once was.

Why do I tell you the story of Persis and Cyril? The emotions we felt in Antioch for Persis and Cyril are surprisingly similar to the emotions we feel here in the Kingdom as we watch the daily life of many believers on earth. For every person who comes to the Lord, our hearts are warmed by the romance. And for those who wander from the Lord and return to the old ways, we cry the tears of Paul. *For, as I have often told you before and now say again even with tears, many live as enemies of the cross of Christ* (Phil. 3:18).

Imagine that. Becoming an enemy of the very cross that purchased your salvation. Note the word *enemy*. It can't be emphasized too strongly. Enemy. An adversary. A hostile force. One who attacks, seeks to injure, or overthrow the victory of the cross. A friend of Satan.

How do you know whether you're living as an enemy of the cross? You know if your mind is set on earthly things, if you're preoccupied with your physical needs and appetites, if you look to the world for approval, if you have tied your identity and your future to a world that is marked for destruction.

These aren't my criteria. These identifying characteristics were listed by the Spirit in our brother Paul's letter to the church at Philippi: *Their destiny is destruction, their god is their stomach, and their glory is in their shame. Their mind is on earthly things* (Phil. 3:19).

Contrast this with those who live as loyal citizens of the Kingdom and who eagerly await a Savior from there: Their minds are set on Kingdom things. They're preoccupied with their eternal needs and spiritual appetites. They look to the Lord for approval. They've tied their identity and their future to God's eternal Kingdom.

How sad it is for us to watch as people who have wed themselves to the Lord of Love through salvation become unfaithful and seek affection, comfort, and approval in the arms of a former lover. Just as Cyril did.

Is this comparison too strong? Not according to our brother, the Apostle James. He agrees with Paul: *You adulterous people, don't you know that friendship with the world is hatred toward God? Anyone who chooses to be a friend of the world becomes an enemy of God* (James 4:4).

Seduced by the world, those who return to her charms often don't see their dalliance with the world as a betrayal of the Kingdom. But it is.

By placing a priority on physical things, you abuse the Spirit within you through inattention and neglect. Your actions fly in the face of the Lord's example on the cross that you die to yourself and live to Him.

By seeking approval from a sinful world, you heap shame and disgrace on your Lord who has openly expressed His dying love for you on the cross. It's your proclamation to a fallen world that Jesus' love was not sufficient for you. If it was, why would you seek comfort in the arms of another?

And when you tie your fortunes once again to a realm that is marked for destruction, you exchange the joys of the Kingdom for the sensations of the world.

When you do these things you become an enemy of the cross and everything it stands for. There is nothing sadder for us than to watch a citizen of the Kingdom give comfort and aid to the enemy.

I wish I could tell you that Cyril realized his error and returned to Persis, his wife who loved him so. But he didn't. He died in a drunken fight. None of his old friends or girlfriends mourned for him. His name became a warning of a ruined life to children and young men.

And I wish I could tell you that all those who wander from the Lord realize their error and return to Him before it's too late. Some do. Many don't. For those who don't, we weep the tears of Paul.

Praying for you,
Theodora

# Curse You, James Dean

## Jared

Loved ones,

Curse you, James Dean. Because of you, generations of American kids wasted their lives trying to be cool. I was one of them.

Every morning for six years the first thing I saw when I woke up was the promotional poster for *Rebel without a Cause*. There you were. Slumped against a brick wall, your leather jacket pulled open showing a white T-shirt; your jeans were cuffed and your legs were crossed indifferently at the ankles; you had one hand on your hip while the other listlessly sported a cigarette. You were the epitome of cool. And, as with all your posters, your brooding expression advertised that somber was in style. For generations of youth, it became a sin to grin.

I remember how I'd practice being cool. Using your poster as though it was a mirror, I'd stand in front of it and slump against my closet door. Then I'd pull open my corduroy coat to reveal a rather meager field of cotton white. With my ankles crossed, my right hand on my hip and a pencil wedged between the fingers of my left hand, I let my jaw grow slack and I brooded. And for a few moments—with a little imagination and as long as no one came in my bedroom and caught me—I knew what it was like to feel cool.

While it was difficult to be cool alone in my room, it was near impossible to maintain that cool outside the room. Still, I tried. I walked with a slow shuffle, indifferent and cocky all at the same time. I spoke in a low, hushed voice (no small feat when you're going through puberty). And above all, I kept my emotions in check, because it wasn't cool to laugh out loud or to show joy or sorrow. When you're cool the only valid emotion is brooding.

After all, I wasn't a kid anymore. Only little kids run to their daddies, or cry when their hamster dies, or jump on their beds, or stay awake for hours Christmas Eve because they're too excited to sleep. Little kids know nothing of cool. And James, you and I were cool. Never mind that our coolness came at the cost of joyful living.

Do you know that I was an adult before I finally took my emotions out of mothballs? At first I thought people would think I was a grinning monkey, but it felt good and I found that it changed my whole attitude and the attitude of those around me. And then—I'm not ashamed to admit it now—I gave myself permission to shed a few tears when my three-year-old daughter sang her first solo in a church production: "This Little Light of Mine." I thought for sure people would think I was a blubbering fool. But they didn't. Forgive me, James, but by then being cool no longer seemed important to me.

Then, a sequence of events occurred that made me realize how foolish I'd been. It began during a men's Bible study. We were studying the Book of Acts. It was the first time I'd ever heard of the preacher named Apollos.

And a certain Jew named Apollos, born at Alexandria, an eloquent man, and mighty in the scriptures, came to Ephesus. This man was instructed in the way of the Lord; and being fervent in the spirit, he spake and taught diligently the things of the Lord, knowing only the baptism of John.

Acts 18:24–25

The characteristics of this man of God struck me. Eloquent. Mighty in the Scriptures. Fervent in the Spirit. *Fervent.*

Wasn't fervent the opposite of cool?

Then we came to chapter 22. Our brother the Apostle Paul was giving his testimony.

I am verily a man which am a Jew, born in Tarsus, a city in Cilicia, yet brought up in this city at the feet of Gamaliel, and taught according to the perfect manner of the law of the fathers, and was zealous toward God, as ye all are this day.

Acts 22:3

Zealous toward God.

Again, this was not cool.

You know how when something catches your attention how all of a sudden you see it everywhere? That's the way it was for me. From that point on it seemed that I was constantly coming across men of God who were anything but cool, including the Master Himself. There was the incident of Jesus turning over the tables of the moneychangers in the temple court: *And his disciples remembered that it was written, The zeal of thine house hath eaten me up* (John 2:17).

From there it was a tidal wave. Our brother and preacher John Knox crying out, "Lord, give me Scotland or I die!" The passionate Puritans risking starvation and disease to find a land where they could worship God freely. The zeal of Wycliffe and Tyndale and Miles Coverdale and others who made it possible for us to read the Bible in English. The heroes of Hebrews chapter 11, those of whom the world was not worthy. Annie Johnson Flint, who was so afflicted with arthritis that she could not play the piano without pain, yet she composed such passionate songs of worship and praise. And the countless thousands who have crossed to this side of the veil, each with his or her own story, each of them zealous, fervent, passionate for the Lord.

If there's one thing I've learned, it's this: Christianity is not cool.

If I had to describe the people with whom I'm now living in one word, the word would not be cool, but exuberant.

Oh my, wait until you hear Jesus laugh, or get a bear hug from the Apostle Paul, or hear Augustine tell a joke, or see the Apostle John's eyes tear up at the news of another convert, or hear Mary, the mother of Jesus, sing an old hymn, or watch the way Luther and Calvin rib each other.

And music? You haven't begun to live until you've heard the laughing and shouting and tears that accompany Fanny Crosby's singing while she's accompanied by Annie Johnson Flint and a band of angels, or until you've heard a cantata written by King David and arranged and conducted by Johann Sebastian Bach.

I can't begin to describe the emotions you're going to feel once you come home. All I can say is that heaven is too hot to be cool.

Let me tell you, having experienced them both, I'll choose Christian exuberance over James Dean and cool any day.

Too zealous to be cool,
Jared

# Living in Light of Eternity

## of Eternity

*Kingdom Traits*

# Identity Confusion
## Dr. Everett Parker

Beloved,

In my day a person's identity was a matter of life and death. We were at war and it was not uncommon for a person to be challenged at a roadblock or by a picket. "Who goes there?" was a daily question, and failure to identify oneself could result in arrest or being shot. Believe me, when a rifle is aimed at your chest the last thing you want is for there to be any confusion about your identity.

Yet there seems to be much confusion among believers on earth as to the necessity of maintaining a distinct identity. This is troubling.

Mind you, the confusion is limited to earth. The Lord knows who are His. As for those of us who have reached this level of existence, we have a heightened perception when it comes to spiritual matters. How can I explain it to you?

Think of a hunting dog. I once was told that a hunting dog can identify a scent as easily as we identify colors. To extend the analogy, a hunting dog following a scent would be like us following a streak of blue on the ground. Even so, spiritual perception is clearer for those of us who live on this side of the veil. It is with this heightened perception that I advise you in this matter of identity.

I begin with a question: What does it matter that people recognize us as believers? Isn't it enough that our Lord knows those who are His? For salvation, yes. In this, we don't need to prove ourselves to anyone.

However, once we are His, God calls us to march under His banner. There are no undercover spies in God's army. Nor is the cause of the Kingdom advanced by those who speak, act, and live like the enemy. Make no mistake about it. You live in the midst of intense spiritual warfare. Battle lines are drawn. Sides are chosen. This we see with alarming clarity.

So then, what does it mean to march under the banner of Christ? The columns of those who do are living proof of the power of the resurrection to change lives. After all, isn't this the essence of Christianity? Change. Before and after. Once I was lost, now I am found. *Therefore if any man be in Christ, he is a new creature: old things are passed away; behold, all things are become new* (2 Cor. 5:17).

Conversely, how is the cause of the Kingdom advanced if the lives of those under the banner of Christ are just as empty, just as unhappy, as the rest of the world? Where is the power of our message if our goals are just as materialistic as our neighbor's? If our children are just as godless? If our marriages are just as troubled? If there is no difference between us and them, then Jesus profits us nothing.

The difference in our lives is a testament to the power of a resurrected Lord. Every godly change is an insignia that identifies us with Him. Every good deed identifies us with our Commander.

In the early days of Christianity, there was no confusion as to whose side Polycarp was on. He lived in the days when the warfare against the Kingdom took the form of a great political persecution. Because of Polycarp's influence over so many, the Roman authorities ordered his arrest. Polycarp was hunted down and dragged into an arena.

He was given a chance to change sides, to deny publicly that he was a follower of Christ and to affirm his allegiance to Rome. If he did so, his life would be spared.

Polycarp refused.

The authorities persisted. What harm would it do to declare that Caesar was his Lord? They appealed to his advanced age. No one would think less of him. People would understand.

Finally, Polycarp had enough of their badgering. He said, "If you imagine that I will swear by Caesar, you do not know who I am. Let me tell you plainly, I am a Christian."

Polycarp raised the banner high. No identity confusion here. His actions remind us that there is a distinctiveness about being a Christian.

Our brother, the Apostle Peter, spoke of this distinctiveness. He said, *But you are a chosen people, a royal priesthood, a holy nation, a people belonging to God. . . . Once you were not a people, but now you are the people of God* (1 Peter 2:9–10).

85

What are the defining characteristics of this chosen people?

We follow a higher authority. Even though you live far from home, you are still citizens of the Kingdom.

We speak differently. Those who march under Christ's banner aren't always talking about themselves. We don't boast, except in the grace of the Lord. We don't make promises we can't keep. We let our yes be yes, and our no, no (Matt. 5:37).

We don't share the same values as the world. We are more interested in relationships that appreciate rather than in things that depreciate (Matt. 6:19).

And we wear proudly the identification badge of the believer. This, above all else. What is this badge, you ask?

Jesus presented it to His disciples on the last night He broke bread with them. It's easy to remember. Three words:

*Love one another.*

Three times that night Jesus commanded His disciples to love one another. "As I have loved you," He said, "so you must love one another." And then, He said, "All men will know that you are My disciples if you love one another."

All men will know. This one thing is what identifies us with Him. Our very identity is at stake. Fail in this and the world will never believe we belong with those who march under the banner of Christ.

The world has posted a sentry.

"Halt! Identify yourself!"

When you answer, will there be any doubt as to whose side you're on?

Your fellow countryman,
Everett Parker, M.D.

# New Eyes
## Theodora

Beloved,

One of the best things about Kingdom living is the personal interaction you have with people you've read about or heard about all your life. You can ask them questions about how they felt when such and such happened, what they were thinking, and if they had to do it over again, would they do it differently?

And then there's the interaction between the people themselves, little things not recorded in the Holy Scriptures. Take the disciples, for example. If you want a fun time, get them together. The anecdotes don't stop! These fellows love to tell stories on each other. And the stories they tell about Jesus . . . the things He'd say to them privately, just Him and them . . . I get gooseflesh just thinking about it. Well, all I can say is that our brother John was right when he said the world couldn't contain all the books that could be written about the things Jesus did and said.

Just the other day I was having a private conversation with our brother, the Apostle Peter. Whenever I get one of the disciples alone I like to ask them questions of a personal nature, the kind of question you wouldn't embarrass them with while sitting around supping.

I said, "What was the greatest lesson you learned while you were with Jesus on earth?"

(Now that might not seem like a really personal question to you, but from experience I've learned to be careful around these fellows. You never know what they're going to say!)

Peter's reply intrigued me. He smiled a brotherly smile and said, "The greatest lesson was also the most difficult lesson."

That got my attention. I sat at his feet, assuming the role of a student. His smile widened when he saw I wasn't going to let him go without an explanation.

"It was at Bethsaida," he said. "We were passing through the town when some of the townspeople came out to greet us. Apparently, word of Jesus' approach had preceded us. The townspeople brought a blind man to him.

"Jesus, seeing that a crowd was gathering, and not wanting to make a public spectacle of him, took the man by the hand and led him out of the town.

"The Master led us to a clearing beside a small patch of sycamore figs. He spit on the man's eyes, touched them, then asked him if he saw anything. The man replied he saw trees, as men walking around."

I grinned at the description.

"Jesus touched the man's eyes a second time and his sight was fully restored. He saw everything clearly now."

Peter reflected for a moment silently and I remember thinking how exciting it must have been to witness a part of the created order responding obediently to the Creator's touch. Apparently, I was reveling too much.

"Don't miss the point!" Peter cried. "Think! Could the Master have cured the man with a single touch?"

I shrugged hesitantly, "Yes, I suppose . . ."

"With a spoken command?" Peter pressed.

"Yes."

"From a great distance?"

"Of course. He's the Master."

"Exactly! So why the two touches?"

"To make a point."

Peter grinned. He nodded. "To make a point . . . but, what point?"

He looked down at me. I looked up at him. Was he expecting me to answer? I had none to give him!

"We were at Capernaum," Peter said, launching into another remembrance. "It was the Sabbath and Jesus had taught at the synagogue. My mother-in-law became ill. The Master insisted on seeing her. He healed her."

"Then word got out," I said.

"And people started coming to the door, bringing their sick, all of them wishing to see Jesus."

A distant look came to Peter's eyes as he remembered that day. He shook his head slowly in wonder of it all.

"So many of them," he mused. "Old Jotham, the butcher. He brought his son, Gaal, who was born with a twisted foot. And Merab, so badly burned when her house caught fire. And Akim. And Hannah . . . fevers, rashes, cuts . . . so many needing to be touched by the Master."

"And then darkness fell," I said, "and some had to be sent home."

"You know this story, do you?" Peter said, grinning. "This part of it."

"Then you know, come morning Jesus was missing."

"His morning prayers," I offered.

Peter nodded. "We found Him down by the lake. By then, there must have already been twenty people waiting for Him at the front door."

"He didn't return to Capernaam with you."

"No, He didn't. He said, 'Let us go somewhere else—to the nearby villages—so I can preach there also. That is why I have come.'" Peter paused. "He turned His back on all those people waiting for Him. Left them standing there. Michael . . . Hoshea . . . Asher . . . Miriam . . . Every one of them with a serious physical need. He alone could help them. Yet, He walked away. I remember being angry with Him. Furious. How could He do something like that?"

"You didn't understand."

"Not until Bethsaida."

"The second touch," I said.

Peter nodded. "At Capernaam I was like the blind man after the first touch. My eyes had been opened to spiritual things, but I wasn't yet seeing clearly, men moving like trees."

"You weren't looking at things through Kingdom eyes."

"I was still looking at things from the world's point of view. I looked at them spiritually, but I was still rooted in the world. I was walking on the edge of understanding, sort of like obeying a parent's instruction, but not understanding the reason behind it."

"While the Master saw things through Kingdom eyes."

"Exactly. He could have healed those people. He could have spent all His days healing people and never done what He came to do."

"And every one of them would have died later."

"While I was still looking at things as though life on earth was the sum total of existence, Jesus saw their real need. He chose to delay their healing until He could heal them permanently and give them a life that would never end."

"You were spiritually sensitive, but not Kingdom sighted."

"Like seeing men, walking as trees."

"But then you got your Kingdom eyes."

"The second touch," Peter said.

I wanted to share this exchange with you, because I can still remember what it was like to live a spiritual life, yet not see things through Kingdom eyes. There were times I was furious with God. Times when it seemed God didn't care, or understand, or that He'd forgotten all about me and the world.

Oh, if you only knew! Just saying these things . . . remembering these thoughts. How foolish. How arrogant. Seeing what I see now . . . I feel ashamed for ever having thought this way.

But I'll suffer the shame for your sake, only pray that God will touch you again and give you new eyes, Kingdom eyes.

I can see clearly now,
Theodora

# 16

# The Standard

## Dr. Everett Parker

Beloved,

Once there was a young lad who came running through the house yelling for his mother.

"Mother! Mother!" he cried. "I'm six feet tall!"

"How did you come to that conclusion?" his mother asked with a smile, for he was just a small boy.

"I measured myself!" he said proudly.

"Oh?" his mother asked. "And what did you use to measure yourself?"

"I used my shoe, and I'm six feet tall!"

Obviously the boy was confused. He'd mistaken the size of his own foot for the unit of measurement we call a foot. While we laugh with amusement at the boy, the fact is there are many people who establish their own standards of measurement by which they determine truth.

Scientists tend to do this. They have determined that truth lies within the range of things that can be observed and measured with the five senses. What of the things that lie outside the boundaries of this standard? What about things that must be taken by faith? Scientists dismiss them outright. In so doing, they ignore or refuse to consider data that may very well have a bearing on their studies.

They've created their own limited standard by which they search for truth. They're using their own shoe to measure the universe.

Not only does truth vary among scientists, philosophers, and theologians, but also among nations. Truth, in the form of laws and customs, varies from country to country because it is based on a people's history, government, and founding documents. What is legal in France may be illegal in England. What is socially acceptable in South Africa may be a *faux pas* in Japan.

As with other kingdoms, the Kingdom of God is not without its laws and guidelines, its standards. However, the authority upon which these Kingdom laws rest is not limited like those of scientists or a product of the past like other countries. It's authority is the God of all creation.

I write this to you who are citizens of the Kingdom. While you are away from home, living in other lands, it's only natural that you encounter ways and customs and laws that are acceptable among the people of those lands. However, their ways are not your ways. Whether you are here or there, you are a citizen of the Kingdom and should govern your lives accordingly.

Our brother, the prophet Amos, received a creative object lesson revelation from God about this matter:

93

Thus he shewed me: and, behold, the Lord stood upon a wall made by a plumbline, with a plumbline in his hand. And the LORD said unto me, Amos, what seest thou? And I said, A plumbline. Then said the Lord, Behold, I will set a plumbline in the midst of my people Israel.

Amos 7:7–8

God had set the standard of what was straight and true and that which was crooked. Even so, He has established the plumb line of truth and righteousness through His Word and the work of His Son. Every saying, every writing, every teaching, every practice, every custom is measured against that plumb line.

And do you think there will be a different plumb line once you pass through the veil and come home? Most assuredly not. Those who live according to the eternal truth of the living God feel comfortable coming home. How many times have I heard new arrivals say, "This feels so natural. So right."

And so it is.

And so I say to you who are beyond the veil, remember who you are. Remember your heritage. Be proud that you are Kingdom-dwellers away from home for a time. Someday you will return and everything will be clearer, cleaner, brighter, with more known than unknown. Until that day comes, remember you are representatives of the Kingdom of the Almighty God.

Dwelling in the truth,
Everett Parker, M.D.

94

# Success

## Jared

Loved ones,

Success is sweet. To pretend otherwise is to deceive ourselves. We desire something. We achieve it. Success.

In my business as a Hollywood screenwriter, success is measured in dollars. Millions of dollars. In 1997 the blockbuster film *Titanic* grossed more than $600 million. Two other films that same year, *Men in Black* and *The Lost World*, grossed $250 million and $230 million respectively. Not as successful as *Titanic*, but still a success.

The yardstick of success for actors is the same as for movies. At one point in his career Harrison Ford signed a movie deal for $25 million for just twenty days of work. That's $1.25 million a day, or $156,250 an hour (for an eight-hour day), approximately $2,600 per minute, or $43 per second. As an actor Harrison Ford is a success.

Businessmen also measure success in dollar values, whether it be cash, property value, or stocks. The more you have, the greater your influence and power, the greater your success.

A pastor friend of mine told me about a funeral he conducted for a successful businessman. He'd never met the man or his family before the funeral. The mortuary introduced them.

The pastor had a standing agreement with that mortuary that if a family needed a minister to conduct a funeral service and didn't have one, he'd conduct the service for them. It was always a difficult assignment because he'd be asked to give the eulogy for a person he'd never met to a roomful of that person's family and friends. So the pastor would spend time getting to know the family before the service so that he could gather facts and anecdotes about the deceased person.

On this occasion no one would talk to him. The businessman's children told him they weren't coming to the funeral, and they didn't. Only a handful of people attended, and the wife made it clear that the only reason she was there was because someone had to sign the papers.

From what little the pastor was able to discover, this businessman had risen to the top of his field by stepping over the carcasses of the people he destroyed on his way to the top. This was the man's legacy, not only as a businessman but also as a father and husband.

Just before he died the businessman made one request for his funeral. His wife vetoed it.

His request?

He wanted a song sung. Frank Sinatra's *I Did It My Way*.

Using the standard yardstick for business, this man was a success.

So was Chris Evert, a tennis champion who began her career at age sixteen. Before she was finished, she won the U.S. Open six times, the French Open seven times, the Australian Open two times, and Wimbledon three times. For seven years she was rated the number one women's tennis player in the world. She had reached the pinnacle of success in her field. On the eve of her retirement, she gave an interview.

"You've achieved the American dream. Number one in the world. What was it like?"

Her response?

She said, "It didn't bring me happiness."

I remember reading that interview. It disturbed me to hear someone say out loud that happiness didn't always accompany success. This was standard fare for Hollywood screenwriters. Fulfill your desires and you'll be happy. This was the essence of the American dream.

Now let's get one thing clear. Kingdom success and the American dream are two different things. The definition of success doesn't change—it is still desire realized. It's the desire that changes. At least, it should. I write this because there is some confusion among believers who are away from their Kingdom home.

There are those who use the standard of the American dream to measure the success of a ministry. They look at the size of the program, the rate of growth, the annual budget, the beauty of the building, and the entertainment value of the singing and preaching to determine the ministry's success. And they smile when the world writes articles about such ministries and interviews the leaders and televises their programs. What they don't seem to realize is that the world takes notice of these ministries only because by its standard, the effort is a success.

By this standard, Walter was a failure as a pastor. He was called to shepherd a small flock of elderly saints in a neighborhood that was gradually being taken over by businesses. His church set no attendance records. They never built a building during his pastorate.

Every time Walter went to a pastor's convention he felt like a failure. Each year he would watch as other men received public accolades for their vision and the growth of their ministries. He listened as the award-winning pastors presented their formulas for success. And every year Walter would try the new formula on his church. It never worked and he wondered what he was doing wrong.

Walter was never invited to preach at the conventions, which was just as well because he didn't have a formula. Besides, who would come to listen to the pastor of a handful of people in a dying neighborhood?

His friends urged him to abandon the small church. It didn't look good on his résumé. Denominational workers advised him to move the church to a location where it had a better chance of growing. But the people in Walter's church were elderly and they couldn't move. And Walter loved them, and they loved him. So he stayed.

Every Sunday they gathered to worship and hear Walter teach them the Word of God. They sang hymns even when the organ wasn't working and their singing wasn't pretty. And they prayed for the missionaries they supported, and for the salvation of their children and grandchildren, and what neighbors remained, and the coming of the Kingdom. In this way they aged together, and one by one they died until there were not enough of them to support the church building, and it was sold.

When it was Walter's turn to pass through the veil that separates time and eternity, guess who was waiting to greet him upon his arrival? Certainly, those of his flock who had preceded him into the Kingdom, but there were others.

Isaiah was there. And so were Jeremiah and Amos and John, called the Baptist. For they too had failed by the world's standards. They knew what it was like to labor for years and not to see an increase. And they wanted Walter to know that he was now in a Kingdom where the measure of a man and his ministry was no longer something that could be recorded in a ledger, but something that was heard. For success in the Kingdom is Jesus saying, "Well done, My good and faithful servant."

Kingdom success has nothing to do with statistics. That's the beauty of it. The Kingdom recognizes the differences of our abilities. For there are those who can start churches, but who can't grow them; who can comfort the sick, but who can't preach; who can organize, but who can't lead; who can construct a church building, but who can't build a church fellowship. Each person is a success when he or she desires to please God.

Obedience is the standard by which success is measured in God's Kingdom. And Kingdom success is the sweetest success of all.

Let me tell you one last thing about Walter. He continues to meet regularly with his congregation. And whenever one passes through the veil, like a good shepherd Walter is there to greet him or her.

Most of the people here have heard of Harrison Ford, but Walter is a celebrity.

Grace and peace,<br>
Jared

# 18

# A Celebrity
## Shankala

Beloved,

A story, like a spark from a fire, can kindle another. That's what happened when I read Jared's last letter. It reminded me of a person who has become dear to me.

To use Jared's words, this man is a celebrity among us though you will not recognize his name because he did not know wealth or power or fame beyond the veil. But he knew Jesus and that was enough for him.

He's from the rolling hills of Wallamo just like me. That's in the country of Ethiopia. He lived there in the 1930s. In those days the Holy Spirit was settin' fires of revival all across the region through the life witness and preaching of new believers. Nana was one of those sparks.

The Word of God was carried to Wallamo through the mountain passes by missionaries. They arrived on the hard clay road that had been packed down for centuries by the feet of merchants and the wheels of their caravans.

The village was little more than a group of huts built with mud and wattle with grass roofs. Windows were open holes in the walls. Unbleached muslin divided rooms. There was little to stop the heat of the day or the cold winds that blew every night.

The missionaries began building huts of their own. Then they set to listenin'. They listened until they understood the language of the people. Then, using simple phrases they began tellin' them about God and His Son, Jesus, the Savior.

One of the villagers believed their message. Then another. And another. Nana, who was a young boy at the time, heard the message through a village elder. He tended the elder's cattle. Nana's older brother also believed, but he was not very strong in the Lord.

Nana's parents were angry when Nana told them that he was worshiping the missionaries' God. They feared the white missionaries and their strange beliefs. They did things to discourage Nana from meeting with the missionaries and their mission church.

For Nana to attend worship services, he had to walk a great distance, but that didn't discourage him. He 'specially liked the early mornin' prayer meetings on Thursdays. To stop him from goin', his parents took away his cloth wrap. Surely he wouldn't be so foolish to travel without his cloth wrap. Neither would they prepare food for him on the days he went to church. But that didn't stop Nana.

*That's not so bad,* he thought, *to miss a few meals in order to hear the Word of God.* So Nana went to the prayer meetings anyway, without food and without his cloth wrap.

When the missionaries saw Nana was naked, they provided another cloth wrap for him, which he kept at

101

a neighbor's house to use on worship days. And so Nana grew in the ways of the Lord.

When Nana learned that Christians thanked God for their food before eating, he wanted to do this too. But his parents forbid him from praying to a strange God before their meals. At first Nana didn't know what to do. *How can I eat without givin' thanks to God who has provided this food for me?* he thought.

After several days of thinking on this, he thought of what he could do. Just before meals he would reach down and scratch his ankles. As he did, he would thank the Lord for his food.

As the months passed Nana's parents grew more and more disturbed about the strange faith that the white people had brought to Wallamo. They thought if they separated Nana from the missionaries, he would soon forget about the strange God of the missionaries.

So they went to the Italians who owned the cotton fields in the lowlands and sold Nana to them. They told the Italians to do whatever they wished with Nana, just not to let him return home.

Nana had heard many fearful stories of the lowlands. The water was bad and many workers came down with malaria. So Nana thought, *I just won't drink any of the water.* But how could he work in the fields and not grow thirsty?

Nana prayed that God would keep him from gettin' thirsty. God answered his prayer. And at the first chance he had, Nana ran away and returned home. He was stronger than ever in his faith.

His parents weren't happy to see him, but they didn't force him to return to the cotton fields. So Nana began attending the missionaries' church again.

Not long after this, Nana's mother became ill and died. This was a sad time for Nana and a time of testin' too. So several of the members of Nana's church attended the funeral service with him, because they knew the elders of the village would expect Nana to honor his mother by wailin' and scratching his flesh. While Nana didn't want to dishonor his mother, neither did he want to return to the practices of his former life.

The elders of the tribe grew angry with him. They threatened him. If he didn't mourn in the proper way something fearful would happen to him.

Nana told them, "I cannot do what you are askin'. It would dishonor my Lord. Jesus is my Savior now and He has given me joy even in a time like this."

Again they threatened him. Again Nana refused to weep and wail and scratch his face.

So the men of the tribe grabbed him and put a rope around the back of his neck, then forward over his arms. They pulled him up on an overhanging branch of a tree and there he hung.

At first, it wasn't too difficult. Nana thought, *I can take this rather than bring shame to my Lord.*

As the afternoon shadows grew long, his body seemed to become heavier and the rope cut into him, makin' deep marks in his flesh. Even though it hurt terribly, Nana didn't think it too much to suffer for his Lord.

A thought came to him. He realized that even though he was hanging from a tree, there was nothin' stopping him from talkin' to the Lord. So while he dangled from the limb of that tree, he prayed and the Lord gave him great joy and strength to bear the pain.

When the sun went down, his father had Nana cut down from the tree. But he was still angry with Nana. So he sent Nana to herd the cows and bring them home in the dark. (This is a great disgrace to anyone in the family during a funeral.)

But Nana didn't mind. *Among the cows I can talk to Jesus,* he thought, *and ask Him to speak to my people and to make me strong for Him.*

Nana's father soon realized there was nothin' he could do to stop his son from following after the missionaries' God. Nana was allowed to move in with the missionaries and work with them. And so he did. And he worked and preached and labored for the Lord until the day God's hand reached through the veil and led him home.

You may ask, Why is Nana so well known in heaven? He wasn't a king. He didn't write a book or compose a song. He had no property. And he didn't come up with any great sayin's that people is repeatin'. To use Jared's word, Nana was no celebrity on earth. So why is he so famous here?

Nana was faithful to God. Everybody in Wallamo knew about the strange God of the missionaries because of what Nana did. And the words he preached continues to be passed from person to person to person so that thousands of people have come to know Jesus because of Nana.

I'm one of them.

I'm in heaven now because Nana spoke to me. He told me about Jesus and I believed him because I could see the love of Jesus in his eyes and hear the love of Jesus in his words and feel the love of Jesus in his embrace and witness the love of Jesus in everything Nana did.

Everyone here has a Nana. I just wanted to tell you about mine.

Forever grateful,
Shankala

# Thinking like an Heir

## Dr. Everett Parker

Beloved,

As a scientist and physician I've always been fascinated by the way the human mind works. A boy's attitude was often the deciding factor that determined whether he would live or die. It also made a difference in how he coped with adversity and pain. The mind is a fascinating part of God's creation.

As a Christian physician, then, I was interested in what the Bible had to say about the mind. One of the better known Scriptures is Proverbs 23:7: *For as he thinketh in his heart, so is he.* This is, of course, compared to what a man says about himself.

But the best fruit of my study of the mind came from the New Testament. What I learned during my earthly walk has now been confirmed during my existence in the Kingdom. And because the way we think determines our identity, I thought it necessary to share my findings with you.

The crux of the matter is this: We are heirs of God's Kingdom and as such, we ought to think like heirs.

At the point of our salvation everything changes. *Therefore, if any man be in Christ, he is a new creature: old things are passed away; behold, all things are become new* (2 Cor. 5:17). This includes our minds.

Our brother, the Apostle Paul, describes this transformation in slavery terms. Before salvation we are slaves to sin (Rom. 7:14). Consequently, we think as slaves. Our lives and choices are fashioned with the goal of satisfying our appetites. This becomes the goal of our lives. After all, so slaves reason, why else would we have these appetites if not to satisfy them?

Slaves can think no other way. Their focus is on this life alone. Possessions and self-gratification become life's goals. Slaves insist on their own way and use other people to accomplish it. They are in a constant state of competition with others for the resources of the earth.

At the point of salvation Jesus breaks the bonds of our slavery. He sets us free. More than that, He adopts us as sons and makes us heirs to His Kingdom.

> Because you are sons, God sent the Spirit of his Son into our hearts, the Spirit who calls out, "Abba, Father." So you are no longer a slave, but a son; and since you are a son, God has made you also an heir.
>
> Galatians 4:6–7

An heir looks at life from an entirely different point of view than does a slave.

> Those who live according to the sinful nature have their minds set on what that nature desires; but those who

106

live in accordance with the Spirit have their minds set on what the Spirit desires. The mind of sinful man is death, but the mind controlled by the Spirit is life and peace.

Romans 8:5–6

An heir lives according to the Spirit. He is empowered by the Spirit of God. He is a child of God. His life of slavery behind him, he lives as an heir to the Kingdom.

What is the earthly point of view of an heir? He recognizes that the world is not his home. He's a citizen of the Kingdom of God. His values, thoughts, desires, goals, and happiness are all tied up in the eternal Kingdom. He sees his life on earth as a small portion of his life, that the best is yet to come. He does not get attached to the things of the world, knowing that their value is at best fleeting. His priorities and values are based on the recognition that he'll live longer in the Kingdom than he will on earth, so any treasures he lays up are heavenly ones.

He no longer has to insist on his own way but desires that the will of God, who is the Master of the Kingdom, is to be done in all things. He no longer needs to be self-seeking but can find fulfillment in making others happy. He has learned to be content in all things, and his mind is free from the worries of this life.

Those who have the mind of a slave cannot understand those who have the mind of an heir. From the slave's point of view, the mind of an heir is unrealistic. And, if life in this world were the only life there was, the slave would be right. The existence of an eternal Kingdom changes everything.

There is a third point of view: that of the confused. These are heirs who have suffered a mental relapse and who once again begin to see things from the point of view of a slave: *Are ye so foolish? having begun in the Spirit, are ye now made perfect by the flesh?* (Gal. 3:3).

Set free from slavery and adopted as sons and heirs to the Kingdom, the confused mind reverts back to the old slavery ways of thinking. It's a common malady. The Apostle Paul had to confront this way of thinking in the churches at Rome, Galatia, Philippi, and Colossae.

It's a pathetic state of mind. Grabbing for the things of this life while hoping for heaven. Battling between the desire to be both generous and greedy. Desiring both the praise of this world and the praise of the next world. Balancing both worlds is a miserable existence.

Our brother, the Apostle Peter, felt the sting of this confused point of view: *But when Jesus turned and looked at his disciples, he rebuked Peter. "Out of my sight, Satan!" he said. "You do not have in mind the things of God, but the things of men"* (Mark 8:33).

Those of us who are writing these letters to you are united in our desire that they can serve as a reminder to you of God's Kingdom of which you are an heir and which each of you will see fulfilled before your very eyes in God's good time. The very existence of the Kingdom puts the world in an entirely different light.

I once had a friend who would give commentary on all the bad things that happened in the world by dismissing it with a phrase, "Well, that's the way things are . . . " I always wanted to correct him by replying, "No, William, that's not the way things are. That's only the way they seem." For there are invisible forces at work that can be seen only by the mind of the redeemed when they look with eyes of faith.

I close this letter with one final Scripture passage that emphasizes the mind of the heir: *And be not conformed to this world: but be ye transformed* by the renewing of your mind, *that ye may prove what is that good, and acceptable, and perfect, will of God* (Rom. 12:2).

A son and an heir,
Everett Parker, M.D.

# 20

# An Open Letter to Vincent Price

## Jared

Dear Vincent,

You got it all wrong.

I have to admit, you had me fooled for years. For me it began on a sticky summer night in Glendora. I was twelve years old and Jimmy Whittler, my best bud, showed me how to sneak into the Big Sky drive-in by squirming under a chain-link fence. We saw a triple horror feature that night. Your *House of Usher* and two others. Vincent, yours was the best movie of the three. I was hooked.

From then on horror flicks became a Saturday staple for us, whether we saw them at the movie houses or drive-ins or on Saturday afternoon TV hosted by Elvira. *House of Wax, The Pit and the Pendulum, The Abominable Dr. Phibes*. I saw them all.

By the time I was old enough to drive, Jimmy and I were taking our dates to all the classics. *Night of the Living Dead*. Low budget. Black and white. A classic. Just for fun, after the movie we'd take the girls to Mt. Hope Cemetery and hide behind the headstones and make weird noises and then scare the living daylights out of each other. We had a lot of first dates in those days.

Then, at USC film school I tried my hand at making an independent horror film. It was a blast. We used all the tricks. A graveyard setting. Morbid-looking headstones and mausoleums. Plenty of dry ice. Plenty of shots through arthritic tree branches. Hands breaking through the sod. And a guy covered in seaweed who walked around on stiff legs. It earned me a decent grade, but it wasn't nearly the quality of horror you achieved, Vincent.

Over the years the constant exposure to the macabre desensitized me to the whole graveyard experience. Then, something happened that not only reawakened old fears, but created a whole new set of them.

Jimmy Whittler died.

For the first time in my life I was forced to face the real thing. This wasn't an actor encased in the coffin. This was Jimmy. And he wasn't pretending. His eyes weren't going to pop open no matter how long I looked at him, and his hand wasn't going to grab me as I walked by. Dead was dead. And it was permanent.

Just a few days before, we had celebrated Jimmy's twenty-first birthday by renting videos of all our favorite horror flicks, including the first one we watched together at the Big Sky drive-in.

Jimmy and I had sort of drifted apart after high school, and he was acting depressed that night. We'd both made it to USC film school, but he preferred keggers to classes. Then, he began shooting up about the same time I was falling for Leslie. News reached me that he was washing dishes at Denny's. Graveyard shift. We got a laugh out of that at his birthday party.

It was his idea to do the video thing. Just the two of us. No beer, no drugs, no talk of film school or Leslie. It was a nostalgia thing. It was also the last time I saw Jimmy alive. He died of a drug overdose two days later.

As I watched them lower Jimmy's coffin into the grave, all I could think of was how cold and stiff he was and that within days his flesh would begin to decay and how we used to talk about those kinds of things and laugh.

A marriage and two children later, my coffin was buried four rows away from Jimmy's. It was one of those unexpected endings to a life. A car accident on the Ventura Freeway just east of the Topanga Canyon exit. I wasn't ready to go. I had screenplays to write. A wife to love. Two little girls to raise—Cassidy, who just turned seven and Erin, age four.

Vincent, it was then that I learned how wrong you were about graveyards.

True, graveyards are not known as happy places. I'll grant you that. The pain of being separated from loved ones is real. But it's also temporary. Vincent, you've done the world a disservice by leading people to believe that graveyards are places to be feared. We shouldn't be afraid of them any more than we are of airports or train stations. For many who depart from this location have a round-trip ticket.

Brothers, we do not want you to be ignorant about those who fall asleep, or to grieve like the rest of men, who have no hope. We believe that Jesus died and rose again and so we believe that God will bring with Jesus those who have fallen asleep in him. According to the Lord's own word, we tell you that we who are still alive, who are left till the coming of the Lord, will certainly not precede those who have fallen asleep. For the Lord himself will come down from heaven, with a loud command, with the voice of the archangel and with the trumpet call of God, and the dead in Christ will rise first. After that, we who are still alive and are left will be caught up with them in the clouds to meet the Lord in the air. And so we will be with the Lord forever.

1 Thessalonians 4:13–17

Did you follow that, Vincent? There will come a day when all the good-byes will be swept away by a flood of eternal joy when the greatest reunion of all time will take place. And it'll take place just a few hundred feet above all the world's graveyards.

Wives will be reunited with husbands, brothers with brothers, parents with children, grandparents and grandchildren. I'll hold Leslie again, and Cassidy and Erin will run into my arms. Oh, what a day that will be.

But then, the day of joy is just beginning. From there we'll walk arm in arm to a table where we will dine with the saints of the ages. It'll be the thanksgiving of all thanksgivings.

Then a voice came from the throne, saying:
    "Praise our God,
    all you his servants,
    you who fear him,
    both small and great!"
Then I heard what sounded like a great multitude, like the roar of rushing waters and like loud peals of thunder, shouting:
    "Hallelujah!
    For our Lord God Almighty reigns.

113

Let us rejoice and be glad
and give him glory!
For the wedding of the Lamb has
   come,
and his bride has made herself
   ready.
Fine linen, bright and clean,
was given her to wear."
[Fine linen stands for the righteous acts of the saints.]
Then the angel said to me, "Write: 'Blessed are those
who are invited to the wedding supper of the Lamb!'"
And he added, "These are the true words of God."

Revelation 19:5–9

Following the dinner we'll attend a funeral. That's right, a funeral. The last one we'll ever attend. I'm looking forward to this one for it will be the funeral of death. *And God shall wipe away all tears from their eyes; and there shall be no more death, neither sorrow, nor crying, neither shall there be any more pain: for the former things are passed away* (Rev. 21:4).

I, for one, am going to shout for joy on the day death dies. And I'm going to walk to the side of that grave and I'm going to stare down into that hole for a long time. Then, I'm going to spit in it, for all the pain it has brought to the world, for separating me from my wife and taking me away from my girls. And then I'll walk away and never think of death again.

So you see, Vincent, you got it all wrong. You're giving graveyards an undeserved bad reputation. Believers need not fear the grave. King Jesus has made it obsolete.

From one who's been there,
Jared

114

# Holding Our Breath
## Theodora

Beloved,

Nearly everyone as they enter the Kingdom is surprised in one way or another. Surprised in a good way. For the most part their comments have a common theme: "It's not at all like I imagined it would be! But then, who could have imagined anything as wonderful as this?"

It takes a while to adjust to some things. For me, it was the sense of breathlessness that permeates our existence. For some reason, I hadn't anticipated having this feeling, but now that I've been here awhile I realize it wouldn't be God's Kingdom without it.

In some ways it's hard to describe. It's anxiety, but in a good sense. It's like being a child again the night before your birthday or a special event. I used to tend an infant girl who, whenever a gift was set before her, would bounce up and down on her toes and shake her hands

115

excitedly in anticipation of opening it. That's the feeling I'm trying to describe.

Everyone in the Kingdom has this feeling, and it never goes away. It exists on two levels. On the one hand we're constantly being surprised in unexpected ways at the wondrous creative expressions of God's love for us—the variety of ways He expresses His love to us is amazing in itself—you'll love it. On the other hand, we're eagerly waiting for the fulfillment of the things He's promised us. To tell you the truth, I don't know which of the two expectations is more exciting.

What are these promises? I'm sure you've heard of them. He's given them to you too. It's just that here, the anticipation of their fulfillment is heightened.

For example, we eagerly wait for the Lord Jesus Christ to be revealed to all the world as the one, true Savior. This expectation is the common hope of all people of God's Kingdom, whether here or away. It is the highest posture that can be attained by a Christian.

The revealing of Christ is the key to solving the mysteries of the ages. It will satisfy people's hearts and enlighten their minds. For those still on earth it is a penetrating light that cuts through the swirling fog of earthly deception.

> For the grace of God that brings salvation has appeared to all men. It teaches us to say "No" to ungodliness and worldly passions, and to live self-controlled, upright and godly lives in this present age, while we wait for the blessed hope—the glorious appearing of our great God and Savior, Jesus Christ.
>
> Titus 2:11–13

Not only do we long for Christ to be revealed, we eagerly wait for the sons of God to be revealed with Him.

116

On that day, it will be clear who are His and who are not. All masks will be stripped away. And those who are His will be transformed, becoming everything God originally intended humankind to be.

I wish I could be more specific, but some things I cannot tell you. It is enough for me to quote our brother, the Apostle John: *Dear friends, now we are children of God, and what we will be has not yet been made known. But we know that when he appears, we shall be like him, for we shall see him as he is* (1 John 3:2).

But I can tell you that once you are transformed into the children of God, you will then be in a position to receive the full blessings that come from such an adoption. This will be done in the presence of the universe, and for this too we eagerly wait. This will be the fulfillment of our grace that was begun at the moment of our salvation.

The only thing I can compare it to is the adoption ceremony that was practiced widely during my time on earth. In such a ceremony a man publicly revealed the heir to his holdings, a person of his own choosing. It didn't have to be a blood relation. The way this was done legally was through adoption.

At the ceremony, the man initiating the adoption gave his heir a ring as a public symbol of his promise of inheritance. In return, when the heir received the ring, he kissed his patron on the cheek and said for all to hear, "Abba, Father."

And so it will be on the day the children of God are revealed. God will assemble the entire universe. Then, His heirs will be revealed and each of us will kiss His cheek and say, "Abba, Father." And the Kingdom of Heaven will be ours. Oh what a day that will be!

There is one more thing that keeps us breathless—the hope of righteousness. This promise will be fulfilled the instant all creation is put right. When sin is removed and all is pure again. When that which is now warped has been restored to its original beauty. No longer will we sing Psalm 73 . . . *But as for me, my feet had almost slipped; I had nearly lost my foothold. For I envied the arrogant when I saw the prosperity of the wicked* . . . for those days will be gone, never to return. On that day and forever, good will prevail and sin will be no more.

There will be a rightness about that day, a sense of peace and finality, a feeling akin to the one that comes with the final chord at the end of a symphony. A sigh of completeness and contentment.

Is it any wonder the Kingdom is holding its collective breath when we are a heartbeat away from the hope of the ages, the climax of creation? My heart skips a beat just thinking about it.

Breathless with anticipation,
Theodora

# Kingdom Weapons
### Dr. Everett Parker

Beloved,

The Civil War was a medical nightmare. To be a hospital patient was to be forced to accept odds as high as ten to one that you would die. And probably slowly. And in agony.

It truly amazed me the creative means people devised to kill and maim. Six-barreled Gatling guns that fire six hundred rounds of ammunition a minute. Howitzers. Mortars that lob 218-pound shells two and a half miles. But the most destructive by far was the common Springfield musket and the minié ball, a soft lead slug that expanded when it came into contact with its target, causing horrific injuries, destroying bone and tissue beyond any hope of repair.

Such is the nature of warfare when nations rise up against nations, and people against people. Their differences can be material, territorial, philosophical, or ideological, but the results are the same. Each side forges weapons with which to destroy the other.

In the cosmos the conflict is spiritual.

> For we wrestle not against flesh and blood, but against principalities, against powers, against the rulers of the darkness of this world, against spiritual wickedness in high places. Wherefore take unto you the whole armour of God, that ye may be able to withstand in the evil day, and having done all, to stand.
>
> Ephesians 6:12–13

There is a battle that has been raging since before the beginning of time. It is real. It is deadly.

The last major battle was fought and won by Jesus, the Savior, on the cross. That sealed it. The end is in sight. However, until He leads His armies back to earth to claim what is rightfully His, small skirmishes continue. That's why it's important that we arm ourselves with the weapons of the Kingdom of God lest we suffer the slings and arrows of the other side needlessly.

What are the weapons of the Kingdom of God?

Like most armies we have our big guns and our everyday weapons. The big guns are the written and spoken word. The Apostle Paul was armed with this weapon. His preaching and teaching and writing greatly advanced the Kingdom on earth. Augustine was another who knew how to use this weapon. His recorded thoughts helped shape the doctrines of generations of believers. And then there were Wycliffe and Tyndale who gave us the Word in the form of the English Bible. These men and others were the thirteen-inch mortars of God's Kingdom. When they fired, the world took notice.

There were also the weapons of the common soldier in the field. The weapons they fired didn't make as much noise, but entire battles have been won with these weapons in the hands of courageous believers. One such weapon is the weapon of kindness.

Barnabas was an expert with this weapon.

When the early church in Jerusalem received reports of the Gentiles coming to know Christ in Antioch, they decided to send an emissary to assess the situation. Mind you, this was an explosive situation. They needed someone who was mature. Rooted in the faith. Someone who could evaluate the situation accurately and report back to them. They chose Barnabas.

It was a wise choice. Not only did he report the situation, but he endeared himself to the people at Antioch. For when a list of the city's prophets and teachers was made, Barnabas was mentioned first (Acts 13:1).

It was Barnabas who sought out Paul and brought him to Antioch. Not many people would be willing to bring in a personality with the strength of a Paul, one who would most certainly overshadow them. Barnabas did.

But of all these things, do you know what always impressed me most about Barnabas? His name. It was a nickname. His given name was Joseph. Nicknames are something that you earn. A certain characteristic becomes so prominent that people begin associating you with the characteristic. There was a boy who grew up in Cairo, Illinois, the same time as my sons. His nickname was Skunk. You can guess why.

Well, Joseph's nickname was Barnabas, which means "son of encouragement." The man was known for his kindness toward others.

While it was men like Paul who fashioned the Christian cause in history, it was men like Barnabas who made it work in the home and in the marketplace.

As you know, there came a time as Christianity grew that it became a threat to the mighty Roman Empire. Once again kingdom lined up against kingdom. Weapons were brought to bear. Rome mobilized her armies and passed laws and used force and torture and intimidation. The Kingdom of God responded with an army of men and women like Barnabas, who were armed with goodness and kindness.

Rome never had a chance.

I realize this has been a roundabout way to make my point. But if I began this letter by saying, "Kindness is one of God's Kingdom traits. Be kind," you probably would have paid little attention to me and I would have done a disservice to the power of kindness. For indeed, it is a weapon of the Kingdom, and it was a major factor in toppling the mighty Roman Empire. While the big guns blazed with their preaching and their words, the everyday skirmishes were fought and won by simple acts of Christian kindness in the heart of Rome, Antioch, Ephesus, Alexandria, and Jerusalem.

I was witness to one such skirmish when a woman, armed only with Christian kindness, won a significant battle against a formidable enemy.

Her name was Sally Berry. She was a volunteer nurse. Untrained in medicine. Middle-aged. Her hair, pulled back, had a splash of gray near the temples. She was a good-natured woman, a widow, having lost her husband in the war six months earlier.

It wasn't uncommon for women to volunteer to work in a field hospital, but it was uncommon for them to volunteer twice. Once they saw the boys lying in soiled straw, the severed limbs, the massive infection; once they heard the moans and cries and sobs, rarely did they return the next day.

Sally was different from the other women. She came back. Day after day. Month after month. She was given all the tasks the doctors and nurses didn't want to perform themselves. There's no fancy way to describe it. Messy. Smelly. Gut-level nursing. Sally performed her duties without complaint.

She was always smiling or humming. She would play dominoes with the boys. Or read their letters to them. Or read to them from books. She always had one condition, though. For every letter or chapter she read, the boys had to promise they'd listen to one chapter from the Bible.

The incident to which I've referred happened shortly after the battle of Stones River. Along with wagonloads of our boys, we also got a belligerent Southern corporal who didn't have the good sense to know to keep his mouth shut. He cursed everyone and everything in sight. Some of it was the pain talking—he'd taken a minié ball to the left leg, and there was heavy bone and tissue damage—but most of it was murderous hatred. You could see it in his eyes.

Normally in a situation like this we'd amputate the leg and send him off to a prison ward. But somehow this boy got hold of a Colt revolver. And when the surgeons came for him, he brandished it, yelling that they were never going to cut off his leg.

Before you could take a deep breath there were four guards in the tent pointing their rifles at his chest. We were about to have our own battle right in the middle of a field hospital tent. To make matters worse, the other patients—Union soldiers all—began yelling, "Shoot him! Shoot him! Shoot him!" After all, he was a Reb.

All of a sudden Sally stepped between the Southern corporal and the four guards. There she stood, calm as you please, with the Reb's pistol pointed at her back staring into the barrels of the four guards. She ordered the guards to leave, saying that they were interrupting her in her duties. Then she turned to the corporal.

"Is that any way to treat your hosts?" she demanded. "How would you feel if one of your guests pulled a pistol on you in your own house? You'd have every right to be outraged. Now put that gun down."

"I won't let them take my leg," the corporal said.

"Nobody's going to take your leg," Sally told him.

He didn't lower the gun. "I don't believe you," he said.

Sally looked him in the eye. She was deadly earnest. "I give you my word," she said.

Whether he took her at her word or whether his strength gave out, I couldn't tell, but next thing I knew the Reb corporal lowered his gun. Sally took it from his hand and began to clean him up.

After a few minutes the Reb lost consciousness.

About a half hour later a litter was sent for him. A table and a surgeon were ready to take his leg. Sally refused to let the litter carriers take the Reb. I was occupied with another procedure but had a clear view of the entire incident. When the litter bearers came back empty, the surgeon went for the man himself. Sally informed him the corporal did not wish to have his leg removed. The surgeon flushed with anger and when he moved toward her, she snatched up the corporal's revolver and held him off.

"I promised him that no one would take his leg," she said calmly.

All manner of abuse was heaped on this poor woman, but nothing could convince her to hand over her patient. She was reminded he was the enemy, that given the chance he would have shot her too only he was too weak to pull the trigger. She was told she was only a volunteer nurse and she had no authority to make a surgical decision. But no matter what they said, she held her ground.

Finally the surgeon said, "Give me one good reason why you're doing this."

Sally smiled and said, "Do good to them which hate you, Luke chapter six, verse twenty-seven."

For three days Sally never left her patient's side. She spoke to him in a whisper, though he never showed any sign of hearing her. She bathed him. Combed his hair. Read the Bible to him. At times she resembled a little girl caring for her doll because he was limp and unresponsive. At other times she would spend ten or twenty minutes whispering into his ear. She spoke so low nobody could hear what she was saying.

News of this peculiar pair spread throughout camp. People would stand at the tent opening and watch her care for the unconscious Confederate corporal.

Then, after three days, his eyes opened. He was unable to move or speak, but it was clear the way he looked at things and tracked them with his eye movement that he was aware of his surroundings. At first he kept looking down at his wounded leg. Sally assured him he still had his leg.

For the better part of a day he followed Sally with his eyes. She would talk to him. Sing to him. Care for him and read to him. Then, he mouthed his last words. Catching her eye, he looked up at her and said in a hoarse voice, "Thank you."

He died shortly after that.

When they came for the corporal's body, the tent was strangely quiet. Respectful. Everyone kept looking at Sally. Her expression was unchanged. Pleasant. Happy.

And after they removed the corporal's body for burial, she went home. We wondered if we'd ever see her again.

Come next morning, there she was, as always. Doing her duty just like she had always done, just like the three days with the Confederate corporal had never happened.

I can't say I was surprised when I met up with the Confederate corporal on this side of the veil. To hear him tell it, there was a whole other battle going on during the three days he lay in that field hospital. He was the enemy in more ways than one. Not only was he a Confederate, but in his disillusion for life he'd become a soldier of darkness long before he was wounded.

During those three days, Sally mounted an attack against everything he'd believed. She leveled a barrage of kindness and love at him the likes of which his defenses had never seen. She breached his defenses and brought a light to the darkness of his mind.

"She was unrelenting," he said. "She saved me at the last hour. The only reason I'm here today is because of her persistent kindness."

Kindness is one of the Kingdom's greatest weapons. Never underestimate its power.

With kind regards,
Everett Parker, M.D.

# The Lesson That Can't Be Taught
**Jared**

Loved ones,

Some lessons can't be taught. They have to be discovered. This is one of those lessons.

Our brother the Apostle Paul described this unteachable concept to the church at Corinth by saying: *God loveth a cheerful giver* (2 Cor. 9:7).

Whoa! Okay. Now that you know the topic is giving, some of you are tempted to drop this letter like it was on fire or something. Stay with me. I'm not taking pledges at the end of the letter. But the fact is this—giving is big in the Kingdom. I've never seen so many happy, giving people in one place before. And you know what? Not only is giving fun, it's contagious.

That's the lesson. God loves us to be happy and God loves us to give freely and the two, contrary to popular belief, are not mutually exclusive.

I know. It doesn't make sense. That's why it's a lesson that can't be taught. But once you discover it, watch out. Giving is addicting. And I'm not talking about just a buck or two here and there.

Just before writing this letter I talked with a few people who gave the ultimate gift—their lives. One missionary who went to Africa said, "Did I like my work? No. My wife and I did not like the dirt and primitive conditions. We had rather refined sensibilities. What's to like about crawling into huts through goat's refuse?"

"Then why did you go?" I asked.

He smiled. "Liking or disliking the conditions had nothing to do with our decision to commit our lives to foreign missions. Love constrained us. We wouldn't have been happier anywhere else."

Happy in miserable conditions. What a concept. Now that's cheerful giving.

Christmas is the most giving time of the year, and one of my favorite Christmas movies was *Scrooge*, based on Charles Dickens' *A Christmas Carol*. Of course the story is so well known and has been acted and adapted, I'm sure you know all about Scrooge and his miserly ways and how he discovered the spirit of Christmas through some unusual events. Notice what I said. He discovered it.

Some tried to teach it to him, others tried to shame him into it, but it was a lesson he had to discover for himself. As do you.

Again from our brother Paul, *Each man should give what he has decided in his heart to give, not reluctantly or under compulsion* (2 Cor. 9:7). And we're not just talking offering-plate and pledge giving here. We're talking about everyday giving with the people with whom you live and work.

I discovered the concept from a sermon. The preacher was Roy Angell, a pastor in San Antonio, Texas. In his sermon he told the story of a young man who happened to be a member of his congregation.

The young man came out of a store one day to find a boy admiring his brand-new car. The boy, a teenager, walked around it several times admiring the car's lines. He looked up and saw the young man.

"This your car?" the boy asked.

"Yep."

The boy let out a low whistle as he ran an admiring hand across the surface.

"My brother gave it to me," the young man said.

The boy looked up. Astonished. "He gave it to you?" he cried. "You didn't have to pay for it or nothing?"

"Didn't cost me a cent," the young man said.

"Wow," said the boy, more amazed than ever.

The young man grinned. This wasn't the first time he'd had this conversation about the car. Anticipating what was to come, he said, "Bet you wish you had a brother like that, huh?"

The boy looked up at him, sober-faced. He said, "Naw. I wish I could be a brother like that."

Wow. What an insight.

Let me tell you, after hearing that story my life was never the same. I caught that boy's desire. More than anything else, I wanted to be a brother like that. I wanted to be a husband like that, a father like that.

I discovered the joy that Jesus knew.

*Looking unto Jesus the author and finisher of our faith; who* for the joy *that was set before him endured the cross,*

*despising the shame, and is set down at the right hand of
the throne of God* (Heb. 12:2).

That verse will never make sense to those who haven't
yet discovered giving. But to those who have, life just
doesn't get any better.

> Can't get enough of it,
> Jared

# The Scandalous Christ
### Dr. Everett Parker

Beloved,

The boy was surprised right up to the moment he died. In all the years I treated the dying and wounded, his was one of the strangest stories I heard.

He was young. (Weren't they all?) But this one looked younger than the others though he and all of his buddies insisted he was old enough to enlist. But you could tell by looking at him that this boy had no right going to war. Of course it's no picnic for any of them, but most of them adapt to the forced marches, lack of sleep, wormy food, blazing heat or freezing cold, and the dirt and mud.

Not this boy.

They tell me he belonged in a music conservatory. That he was a harpist. That when he played, if you closed your eyes, you could swear heaven had opened and angels had descended.

It seems that one day the boy'd had enough of war and decided to go fishing. Only he forgot to tell the enemy he was no longer a soldier.

He tied a string to his bayonet, took up a sitting position on the riverbank, and began fishing in the river. From behind the parapet his buddies yelled at him to come back where it was safe. He ignored them, occasionally lifting the string from the water to see if he had a bite.

A rustle of noise came from the Reb side of the river. Then voices and laughter. The sight of a boy fishing between enemy lines amused both sides.

"Is he crazy?" one of the Rebs shouted.

"Never done anything crazy before," came the reply.

"That sure ain't the actions of a sane man," the Reb shouted back.

The boy beside the river gave no indication he heard what they were saying about him. He merely lifted the string from the water to see if he'd caught anything.

For an hour the two sides watched the boy fish. The appearance of officers on both sides changed all that. The jests that were traded back and forth were exchanged for minié balls and soon a full-fledged battle was taking place. The trees grew thick with smoke as bullets flew in both directions. All the while the boy beside the river kept fishing as though it was a lazy summer day on his family's farm.

He seemed genuinely surprised when the first bullet struck him. Reb soldiers splashed across the river and trampled over him. After a time the battle shifted and the Rebs were pushed back across the river, and the boy's buddies found him lying beside the river with his rifle that had the string tied to the bayonet. The boy had been hit twice more; once in the arm, and once in the leg. His eyes were wide with astonishment as though he couldn't comprehend why anyone would want to interrupt him while he was fishing.

That's how he was when they brought him to me. Wounded bad. Astonished. And confused. He died that night right after asking me if I'd see to it that the boys recover the fish he'd caught from the river because fish cooked over an open fire beat hardtack any day.

I'm reminded of that incident when I observe how many believers on earth live their lives, completely unaware that a spiritual battle is raging all around them.

Like the boy who went fishing, they don't want to acknowledge that there's a war going on. Like the boy, they think they can just go about doing what they want to do and ignore the fact that the enemy is advancing. And, like the boy, they're just as surprised when they or someone they know gets wounded in the spiritual crossfire.

Pretending something isn't so doesn't change reality.

Finally, my brethren, be strong in the Lord, and in the power of his might. Put on the whole armour of God, that ye may be able to stand against the wiles of the devil. For we wrestle not against flesh and blood, but against principalities, against powers, against the rulers of the darkness of this world, against spiritual wickedness in high places. Wherefore take unto you the whole armour of God, that ye may be able to withstand in the evil day, and having done all, to stand.

Ephesians 6:10–13

Looking all doe-eyed when the slings and arrows of the evil one fly all about you is not your strongest defense. Heed the warning of our early teachers:

Be sober, be vigilant; because your adversary the devil, as a roaring lion, walketh about, seeking whom he may devour: Whom resist stedfast in the faith, knowing that the same afflictions are accomplished in your brethren that are in the world.

1 Peter 5:8–9

If I learned anything during my years on earth, it was that the wise man sees things clearly for what they are. He doesn't try to make them something they aren't.

This goes for the person and work of our Savior, Jesus Christ, as well. There are many who want to remake Him into something He is not. They want to soft-sell His message so it doesn't offend anybody. But the truth of the matter is that Jesus the Christ is an offense to many, and as long as there is sin in the world He will always be offensive to those who live in sin.

Jesus is a stumbling block. An offense. A scandal to those who believe that humankind is basically good, that the world is improving day by day, and that there is no such thing as sin.

Jesus Himself said, *Blessed is he, whosoever shall not be offended in me* (Luke 7:23).

Jesus is saying, "How happy is the person who does not stumble over Me, who is not vexed by Me, shocked by Me, excited by feelings of repugnance by Me." For those who want to pretend sin is not real and the world is not the field of battle for two great spiritual forces, the message and very presence of Jesus is an obstacle to overcome.

Mealy-mouthing His message and pretending it isn't so is just as foolish as fishing at the creek in the middle of a battle. A man cannot lay down his own conditions by which he will enter God's Kingdom.

This is the way:

Jesus saith unto him, I am the way, the truth, and the
life: no man cometh unto the Father, but by me.

John 14:6

And these are the terms:

Then said Jesus unto his disciples, "If any man will come
after me, let him deny himself, and take up his cross, and
follow me. For whosoever will save his life shall lose it:
and whosoever will lose his life for my sake shall find it."

Matthew 16:24–25

You can stumble over it and pretend it isn't so, but
you'll only be fooling yourself.

Blessings,
Everett Parker, M.D.

# 25

# Front Row Seats
## Theodora

Beloved,

It's confession time. I love sporting events. My earthly pastor didn't. He was a strong preacher who more than once railed against such things. I remember clearly one of his sermons:

"Again there are chariot races and satanic spectacles in the hippodrome, and our congregation is shrinking," he thundered. "It is on this account and because I feared and anticipated the negligence which comes from ease and security that I exhorted you and encouraged you in your love not to squander the wealth you had won by fasting, nor to inflict on yourselves the outrage that comes from Satan's spectacles. As it seems, no profit came to you from this exhortation. See how some who heard my previous instruction have today rushed away. They gave up the chance to hear this spiritual discourse and have run off to the hippodrome."

Now, I dearly love our brother Chrysostom. As a deacon of the church, he served me faithfully before being appointed presbyter and chief preacher of Antioch. As a preacher, he was without peer. I learned many valuable truths at his feet. And he was right about many people neglecting their spiritual duty to attend the chariot races. But he didn't much like sporting events in general, and I did. And I didn't see where a Christian had to give up the one for the other. In my opinion, there was time enough for both, each in its own place.

As it turns out, I'm not alone. A good number of us in the Kingdom still love a good sporting event. One of the exciting things about being here is that we get front row seats every time. And best of all, our brother Chrysostom doesn't give me a hard time about it. Probably because at the sporting events I usually sit next to our brother the Apostle Paul. He's a big sports fan.

You probably could have guessed that from his writings. To the church at Corinth where the Isthmian Games were held on the first and third years of the Olympiad, he wrote:

> Do you not know that in a race all the runners run, but only one gets the prize? Run in such a way as to get the prize. Everyone who competes in the games goes into strict training. They do it to get a crown that will not last; but we do it to get a crown that will last forever. Therefore I do not run like a man running aimlessly; I do not fight like a man beating the air. No, I beat my body and make it my slave so that after I have preached to others, I myself will not be disqualified for the prize.
>
> 1 Corinthians 9:24–27

To the churches of Galatia, he wrote, *You were running a good race. Who cut in on you and kept you from obeying the truth?* (Gal. 5:7).

Writing to his beloved Timothy, he said, *Timothy, my son, I give you this instruction in keeping with the prophecies once made about you, so that by following them you may fight the good fight* (1 Tim. 1:18).

And, *Similarly, if anyone competes as an athlete, he does not receive the victor's crown unless he competes according to the rules* (2 Tim. 2:5).

And of himself, he confessed, *I have fought the good fight, I have finished the race, I have kept the faith* (2 Tim. 4:7).

The man loves his sports.

Not long ago we watched an event that we're still talking about. The event was the Special Olympics and the venue was the UCLA track and field facilities. Over 3,200 physically disabled young men and women participated. One race, the 400-meter run, was especially exciting.

A boy with Down's syndrome led the pack from the start, and as they rounded the final turn on the track his feet got all tangled up and he fell in a cloud of dust. Then, something unusual happened. All the other runners stopped, ran over to the fallen runner, helped him to his feet, and would not continue the race until they were convinced he was unharmed.

Let me tell you, we cheered until we were hoarse over that race. There were no losers that day, only winners.

Another event that caused a buzz among us was the tae kwon do competition leading up to the Summer Olympics of 2000. Like the Special Olympics race, this one had us on our feet cheering.

Two best friends, Esther Kim and Kay Poe, were each one victory away from claiming the last spot on the

Olympic team for the United States. As it turned out, they ended up facing each other in the final match.

Both of them had trained all their lives for this moment. Both had dreamed of someday going to the Olympics. But there was only one spot remaining on the team. One of them would make it, the other would be left behind. One friend would eliminate the other.

Under normal circumstances, the two young women were evenly matched. However, in the preceding match Kay Poe had dislocated her kneecap and could barely stand. She would have to compete in the final round injured.

The two women took to the mat. They bowed to each other, then to the referee who would start the bout. Then, the unusual happened. Before a blow was struck, the referee awarded the match to the injured Kay Poe.

The crowd was stunned.

Esther Kim had forfeited. She said she was unwilling to compete against her best friend in her injured condition, even though her decision meant she would forfeit her dream of going to the Olympics.

Kim explained, "I wasn't throwing my dreams away; I was handing them to Kay."

The crowd in the Kingdom stands went wild.

Some people mistakenly believe that there will be no competition in the Kingdom. I can tell you from first-hand experience, they're wrong. In fact, this is the most competitive environment I ever lived in.

There is strong competition to fulfill our brother Paul's teaching in Philippians 2:3–4:

> Do nothing out of selfish ambition or vain conceit, but in humility consider others better than yourselves. Each of you should look not only to your own interests, but also to the interests of others.

139

We try to outdo each other in unselfish acts of love. Believe me, it's fierce competition.

And then there's Kingdom taunting. You can find it described in the sermon called Hebrews: *And let us consider how we may spur one another on toward love and good deeds* (Heb. 10:24).

The way it was described to me, the word translated *spur,* can also be translated *provoke.* To use the vernacular, we're to taunt, incite, rib, stir, and get on each other's case to love more and to perform good deeds.

Like I said, the competition is stiff. Our brother Barnabas is particularly skillful in inciting riots of goodness. Some of us are trying to talk him into opening a training facility.

Kingdom competition. Catch the spirit.

Cheering you on,
Theodora

# 26

# Living Free

## Jared

Loved ones,

Not all prisoners are behind bars. While digging through old books in the library for a research paper in history, I came across the story of a convict who was released after spending twenty-six years on Devil's Island, the notorious French penal colony off the coast of South America.

Years later, of his own volition, he returned to Devil's Island to visit his friends who were still in prison. They asked him what it is was like on the outside.

He shook his head. What most depressed him was the spiritual collapse of society and decline of conscience and intelligence. He concluded: "Not all prisoners are behind bars."

Who better to recognize bondage than a convict? Iron bars aren't the only things that cage us. We can be imprisoned by superstition, hate, fear, guilt, poverty, and even wealth! The irony of the country where I spent my earthly days was that a lot of people lived as prisoners in what was touted as the "land of the free."

One of my last earthly experiences was that of imprisonment. I was on the freeway, driving home, when an erratic driver approached from my blind side traveling over a hundred miles an hour. Swerving across three lanes, he clipped the front end of my car, knocking me into the path of a huge truck.

I tried to hold my lane, but in doing so, I lost control of the car. The next thing I knew it was as though I was in a washing machine during spin cycle. When everything around me finally screeched to a halt, I was dangling upside-down with my seat belt cutting into me.

I couldn't get out of the car. The seat belt was jammed. The doors were squashed. And the steering wheel was pressed against my chest. I was stuck and helpless.

That's when I smelled gasoline. Smoke was already coming from the engine. I felt incredibly tired and weak. All I could manage was a weak yell for help.

I know what it's like to feel trapped. I was imprisoned in that car and helpless to save myself. I needed someone from the outside to break in and save me.

This is exactly what our brother, the Apostle Paul, was describing in Romans 7: *For what I want to do I do not do, but what I hate I do. What a wretched man I am! Who will rescue me from this body of death?* (Rom. 7:15–24).

Trapped. Whether it's physically or emotionally or spiritually, the feeling of helplessness is the same. Who will rescue us?

I needed someone from the outside to save me from the car accident. Firefighters with the jaws of life came to my rescue. Spiritually, there is only One who is on the outside of our prison (One who is without sin) who can help us. All others are trapped just like we are. That person is Jesus.

He announced His intentions to do just that one day when He was preaching in a synagogue in Nazareth. The scroll of Isaiah was handed to him. He opened it and read:

> "The Spirit of the Lord is on me,
>     because he has anointed me
>     to preach good news to the poor.
> He has sent me to proclaim freedom
>     for the prisoners
>     and recovery of sight to the blind,
>     to release the oppressed,
>     to proclaim the year of the Lord's
>     favor."
> Then he rolled up the scroll, gave it back to the atten-
> dant and sat down. The eyes of everyone in the syna-
> gogue were fastened on him, and he said to them, "Today
> this Scripture is fulfilled in your hearing."
>
> Luke 4:18–21

Of course, then He set out doing exactly what He said He was going to do. He went to Capernaum where a man was bound by an evil spirit and Jesus set him free. When He came to a town where a man was bound by social isolation and the physical discomfort of leprosy, Jesus set him free. When He encountered people bound in ignorance and oppressed by the law, Jesus taught them the truth and set them free. When Jesus' close friend Lazarus was bound in funeral cloth and held by death, Jesus resurrected him and set him free. And when Jesus saw you enslaved to your own sin and sentenced to death, He died on the cross and set you free.

That's the good news.

The bad news is that many who have been set free by the Savior continue to live in prisons of one kind or another. Technically they're free, they just don't live as free people. It's as if they've been set free from Devil's Island only to become enslaved by the invisible chains of doubt and fear.

Do you know how difficult it is to free a person who doesn't want to be free?

In the days when I lived on the other side of the veil, it was popular to be a victim. Everyone was a victim of something. Their anger was their parents' fault. They were depressed because of what their boss did to them. They were driven to crime or drink or divorce. Never responsible, always a victim.

It reminds me of the story I heard of the Arabian thief named Akaba. He was a powerful man. Five hundred cohorts took orders from him. He had hundreds of slaves waiting to fulfill his every desire. But Akaba was unsettled. He was getting on in age and he began to worry about his inevitable death.

So Akaba sought out the Arabian chieftan named Ben Achmet, who was renowned for his life of austerity and devotion. Akaba said to him, "Show me what I must do to have a happy immortality." The man of faith led the thief to nearby mountains that were steep and rugged. Pointing to three large stones, he told the thief, "Pick these stones up, and follow me up the mountain."

Laden with the three heavy stones, Akaba could barely move. He cried out, "I can't follow you like this! These stones are too heavy!"

"Then cast one of them down. But hurry, let's be on our way."

The thief dropped one stone but was still barely able to move. "It's still impossible," he said. "You yourself couldn't climb this mountain carrying these two stones."

144

The chieftain looked at him, then said, "Then drop another stone."

Akaba dropped the second stone and with great difficulty began climbing the mountain until, exhausted from effort, he cried out that he could go no farther. The chieftain told him he could drop the last stone. No sooner had the thief done this than he mounted the grade with ease and was soon standing on the summit.

"Son," the man of faith said, "you have three burdens which hinder you on your way to the next life. Disband your troop of lawless plunderers. Set your slaves free. And restore your wealth to its original owners. It's easier for you to ascend this mountain with the three rocks than it is for you to find a happy immortality with the power, pleasure, and riches that are weighing you down."

What a pity that so many believers are like the thief of this story. Set free from the bondage of sin and death, they now carry self-imposed burdens of guilt and anger and meaningless rules.

It's time you dropped the things weighing you down and declared your own personal independence day. If Jesus set you free, you are free indeed. It's time you enjoyed your freedom.

Forever unchained,
Jared

# 27

# Confidence

## Dr. Everett Parker

Beloved,

After reading Jared's last letter, I couldn't help but add a brief comment and story of my own on the subject. The story came to Cairo, Illinois, from Canada. It had to do with the underground railroad, the loosely organized trek by which runaway slaves made their way North to freedom by traveling at night and hiding out in friendly homes during the day. Of course, as soon as they reached Canada they were free.

One of the secret routes actually involved using a train for the last leg of the trip. As it drew into the Toronto station, a woman who had helped countless slaves complete their journey across the border saw one slave, a middle-aged male of good size, still crouching in the corner of the box car. He was afraid he was still being pursued.

"Joe, why are you cowering there?" the woman asked.

He answered with wide, frightened eyes.

"You're a free man on free soil, Joe! Praise God, you no longer have to be afraid!"

Similarly, I have seen boys who were safely behind the lines following a battle curled up in a ball in a corner or on a cot, afraid to accept the reality of their safety.

And I have seen countless Kingdom residents who are forgiven, cleansed, and made righteous before God who—just like Joe and the frightened soldiers—still cower in fear and shame as though their sins were still pursuing them or in some way a danger to them.

Like the woman in Toronto, I want to shout at them, "Why are you cowering there? Praise God, you're free! You're a citizen of God's Kingdom of liberty! You have no reason to fear. You have been granted eternal life and an eternal home that no one can take from you!

*Who shall separate us from the love of Christ? Shall tribulation, or distress, or persecution, or famine, or nakedness, or peril, or sword. . . . Nay, in all these things we are more than conquerors through him that loved us* (Rom. 8:35–37).

*For God hath not given us the spirit of fear; but of power, and of love, and of a sound mind* (2 Tim. 1:7).

Of all people, Christians should walk with their heads held high, not in haughtiness, but in confidence for we are God's chosen people, heirs to the kingdom, and joint-heirs with Christ. Cowering Christians dishonor the sacrifice of the One who saved them.

*For I know that my redeemer liveth, and that he shall stand at the latter day upon the earth* (Job 19:25).

Confident in my salvation and the
Savior who made it possible,
Everett Parker, M.D.

# 28

# Bragging Rights
## Theodora

Beloved,

I'd like to approach a subject that, on the surface, appears to be bad manners. The subject is bragging, or boasting, whichever word you prefer. It's safe to say that nobody likes a braggart, a person who is forever talking about himself. But just because some people abuse something doesn't mean it's wrong.

I'm of the opinion that there are times to boast and that many who are in the Kingdom of God don't boast often enough.

Let me explain.

The Scriptures are clear regarding the evils of personal boasting. *As it is, you boast and brag. All such boasting is evil* (James 4:16). Not only is it evil, it's boorish and painful to listen to.

But there is a time to boast, and reasons to boast. This too is clearly taught in the Scriptures.

*Therefore, as it is written: "Let him who boasts boast in the Lord"* (1 Cor. 1:31).

And why not boast in the Lord? Is there anything greater about which we can talk? He is our righteousness, our holiness, our redemption! He has loosed the pangs of death and purchased our souls with His blood! The angels sing about Him! He is our hope, our joy, our all! King of kings and Lord of lords!

If not for Him we would dwell in darkness, gnashing our teeth on the bitter fruit of our sin, without joy, without light, without hope. Because of His sacrifice we need no longer fear the grave, the due justice of our lives. But we can enjoy life abundant and free!

Tell me then, why should we not boast? Had you a wealthy uncle who cared for you extravagantly, would you not sing his praises? You have a Savior, who loves you more and showers you with a wealth of gifts and joy that you do not deserve. For Him, you keep silent?

And not only should we brag about our Savior, but we should brag about one another. In truth, it saddens my heart when I see Christians critical of each other.

Our brother, the Apostle Paul, was a man of great joy. Listen to how he spoke of his fellow believers:

> For I know your eagerness to help, and I have been boasting about it to the Macedonians, telling them that since last year you in Achaia were ready to give; and your enthusiasm has stirred most of them to action.
>
> 2 Corinthians 9:2

Did you ever consider that by boasting about one another it might encourage others to greater faithfulness? Do you see now why I'm concerned that people consider boasting to be a bad thing? Boasting in the

149

Lord and about the Lord's people praises God and builds the work of the church.

And there's one thing more about which we should boast—our sufferings. *And we rejoice in the hope of the glory of God. Not only so, but we also rejoice in our sufferings, because we know that suffering produces perseverance* (Rom. 5:2–3).

For those of you who did not learn this verse in the same language in which I was taught it, an explanation is probably in order. While some translations have "we also rejoice in our sufferings," the way I learned it was, "we also boast in our sufferings." Actually, it's the same word that was used in the other verses I quoted about boasting.

Odd thing to boast about, isn't it? Our sufferings. Let's keep this in perspective though. We're not supposed to boast about ourselves, remember? So boasting about our sufferings in such a way as to make people feel sorry for us is just a sad way of getting attention.

So then, how should we properly boast about our sufferings? In praise to God. Thanking Him publicly during difficult days, knowing that He can bring good out of all things, and also knowing that our hardship is increasing our spiritual strength, producing perseverance.

If we hang our heads and moan and complain, how different are we from the rest of the world when it encounters hardship? But if we keep our heads high and trust God, we are boasting in a godly way about His care and goodness.

Let me tell you, I think it's far past time that we start bragging—bragging about the greatness of our God, the wondrous love of our Savior, the growth in grace of our fellow believers, and the faithfulness of God to us when days grow dark. That He could take something that would destroy someone of no faith and in us bring about a blessing, why it's nothing shy of a miracle.

Have I managed to convince you that all bragging and boasting is not wrong? If not, just wait until you pass through the veil and see for yourself how much God brags about you.

Bragging about you to others,
Theodora

# 29

# Saint Goody Two-shoes
## Jared

Loved ones,

What's so frightening about Miss Goody Two-shoes that no one wants to be like her? The speed and vehemence with which people distance themselves from this young lady is amazing. One would think she's the carrier of a deadly plague.

How often do you hear, "Well, I'm no Goody Two-shoes." What do we mean by that? Are we saying, "Hey, don't get me wrong, I can sin just as well as the next guy." This is something to boast about?

Nor do we wish to be categorized as a do-gooder, another riddle in my mind. Why are we so concerned that people not mistake us for doers of good? When did doing good become a crime?

Let's address the Miss Goody Two-shoes issue first. She's not the monster people make her out to be.

Mrs. Margery Two-shoes—yes, she got married—was the product of famed playwright Oliver Goldsmith's imagination. Early editions of this rags to riches tale are dated around 1765. The way the story goes, Goody was a homeless child who struggled to make it through life with only a single shoe.

The title page of her story describes the book as a history:

> with the means by which she acquired her learning and wisdom, and in consequence thereof, her estate; set forth at large for the benefit of those

> Who from a state of Rags and Care
> And having Shoes but half a pair,
> Their fortune and their fame could fix
> And gallop in a Coach and Six.

Not exactly a monster, is she? And the "goody" part of her name? It's a contraction for "Goodwife," a form of address roughly equivalent to our "Mrs."

The story of Goodwife Two-shoes has nothing to do with juvenile boasting or syrupy goodness. In fact, her story was a model of honesty and initiative for children for over a hundred and fifty years. Not until 1934 was her name used in a negative, cynical way. Poor Goody. She's been slapped with a bad reputation she doesn't deserve.

Then there's the do-gooder bugaboo.

I heard of a professor who was writing a book that would teach readers how to do good deeds in everyday life. One of his students asked him if it was a work of fiction. A book buyer from a major chain of bookstores refused to buy it if the word do-gooder appeared in the subtitle as planned. And a woman friend who spent much of her time raising money to help the poor and destitute agreed, saying, "No one wants to be called a do-gooder."

Even Webster's dictionary describes do-gooders in less than favorable terms: "an earnest often naive humanitarian or reformer."

This was a puzzle to me until I slipped beyond the veil. Then, I understood. It is not in the nature of humans to do good. It is in their nature to look after themselves, to compete to survive. That's not to say citizens of the earth are incapable of doing good, but they have to overcome their nature in order to do it. After all, "Nobody wants to be known as a do-gooder."

The opposite is true of those who are citizens of the Kingdom of God. It is their nature to do good. Doing good is a hallmark of the Kingdom. At the point of salvation, when we are made citizens and heirs of the Kingdom, a change comes over us. We are a new creation. At that point, the capacity and desire to do good is instilled in us.

The ironic part of all this is that I didn't have to cross the veil before understanding this. It was in the New Testament all along. *For we are God's workmanship, created in Christ Jesus to do good works* (Eph. 2:10).

This whole issue of Goody Two-shoes and do-gooders is one of the clear separations between the citizens of a fallen world and citizens of God's Kingdom. Our good works identify us as citizens of the Kingdom as surely as an Irishman's accent identifies him as a native of the Emerald Isle.

Lord Jesus was a known do-gooder (John 10:32). So was Dorcas, a saint of the early church (Acts 9:36). Jesus gave Himself for us not only to redeem us from sin and purify us but also to equip us thoroughly so that we are eager to do good works (Titus 2:14; 2 Tim. 3:17).

154

The Scriptures are quite clear about this. We are to be known for our good works. They ought to be as noticeable as a light shining in the darkness (Matt. 5:16). They ought to be as hard to hide as another man's sin (1 Tim. 5:25). They ought to be so visible that people who dislike you and speak against you are forced to admit that you are known for your good works (1 Peter 2:12).

Young men of the Kingdom should strive to show a pattern of good works (Titus 2:7). Women of the Kingdom are made beautiful by their good works, not their hairstyle or makeup (1 Tim. 2:10). The currency of the Kingdom is good works. Those who are wealthy in the Kingdom are wealthy in good works, those who are poor are destitute of good works (1 Tim. 6:18).

If there is any competition in the Kingdom, it is the competition to provoke one another to love and good deeds (Heb. 10:24). That should be understood exactly how it sounds. We're to poke or prod each other, to stimulate each other to good works.

Christians are the Goody Two-shoes of the world. We're the do-gooders. It's part of our nature, part of our heritage. Disassociating ourselves from Miss Goody Two-shoes is like disowning a member of the family.

If I could, I'd incite a riot of good works among you, that your heritage might be clearly known to all people and that God would be glorified by your actions.

An unashamed do-gooder,<br>Jared

# Glimpses of Heaven

# Home
## Theodora

Beloved,

You're undoubtedly wondering what home is like. How do you describe the indescribable?

Our brother the Apostle John used several comparisons to describe what he saw. He described home figuratively—as a bride adorned for her husband (Rev. 21:2), as a city with the brilliance of precious gems (21:11), as a garden with fruit and a river (22:1–2), and as a place where we will dine in celebration (19:9).

Jesus our Savior described home to the road-weary disciples as a place with many mansions (John 14:2).

And when our brother the Apostle Paul was caught up into Paradise, he heard certain inexpressible utterances of such grandeur that he was forbidden to describe them to others (2 Cor. 12:3–4).

Such are the glories of our heavenly home. There are things you will expect to see. You'll see them. There are also things you couldn't begin to imagine. Wonderful things. Things for which there are no words, only light and sound and emotion. Earthly comparisons fail us.

So how can I describe home to you in a way they have not? An incident from when I was a little girl might suffice. It was one of the worst days of my life.

My father was away on a buying trip. Grandmother was ill and all of my mother's energies were spent caring for her. So they entrusted me to the care of friends, which delighted me because they had a daughter three years older than me whom I adored. Persis. I couldn't be happier. (Yes, this is the same Persis about whom I wrote earlier.)

Spending the day with Persis made me feel bigger and more grown-up than I was. I would have done anything for her. She was everything I wanted to be when I grew up. Pretty. Confident. Everybody liked her. I followed her around like a pet lamb.

That afternoon her mother sent us to the market to purchase grain for the evening meal. On the edge of the marketplace we encountered Rufus and Apelles who had just come from the hills. They were Persis's age. I can't tell you how grown-up I felt standing there with the three of them.

Rufus told us the two of them had just returned from the hills where they'd come across a pair of lion cubs playing in the niche above the river. Persis insisted they were telling us a tale, but she couldn't shake them from their story.

When the boys left us, Persis turned to me and said, "Let's go see the lion cubs for ourselves!"

The doubt and fear must have shown on my face, because she said, "It'll be alright! We'll just go there, take a look and come right back. No one will know!"

160

The thought of lions terrified me. Even more so the thought of the trouble I'd get into if mother learned I had gone into the hills. It was clearly forbidden. The hills were filled with wild animals and thieves.

Persis knew this too, but seeing lion cubs was too great a lure for her and she was too great a lure for me. So we headed for the hills. I have to confess to feeling a sense of adventure as we waded across the river and began our ascent.

Storm clouds gathered overhead as we reached the rocks. "We'll be home before it rains," Persis said. She kept telling me how brave I was for one so young. I acted brave for her.

It began to rain just as we reached the niche in the rock where the lion cubs were reported to be. The place was a shallow cave scooped out of the side of the hill. We peeked over some rocks from a safe distance. The niche was empty.

Persis was furious. "It's just like boys to lie to us like that!" she said.

We turned to go back home. Just then, a huge horned buck blocked our path. He was twice as large as me. He snorted angrily at us. His eyes were yellow with rage. His cloven hooves pawed the ground.

I never did learn what it was that made him so angry. He may have been a sentry goat protecting his territory, or possibly Rufus and Apelles had thrown rocks at him. But there was no mistaking the fact that he wanted to do us harm.

We turned back and scurried up some rocks just as he began his charge. Halfway up the rock Persis slipped. She turned her ankle and scraped her leg against the rock. The side of her leg was scratched red.

161

Even today I can't tell you how we managed to make it to that tree ahead of the sure-footed buck, but somehow we did. The limbs and the leaves shuddered as the angry buck rammed repeatedly into the trunk.

The rain began to fall heavily.

So there we were, treed by an angry goat who refused to leave us alone just as the heavens opened up. We were frightened and wet. Persis's ankle was swollen twice its normal size. And no one knew where we were.

The day slipped by and still the buck wouldn't leave. He snorted, butted the tree, and paced relentlessly, eyeing us with his yellow eyes.

Our fears rose as darkness fell.

We never knew for sure when the buck finally gave up on us. He would wander off into the darkness and though we couldn't see him, we could hear him snorting. The interval between snorts grew longer and finally we heard nothing at all except the rain pelting the rocks. Even then we were cautious as we climbed down from the tree.

By now it was so dark I could barely see Persis when she was standing beside me. The rain became a torrent. Lightning pierced the black clouds. A thunderous refrain followed. The rocks shivered in the jagged white light. So did I.

Though we weren't far from the city, traveling was treacherous. Between flashes of light, darkness blanketed everything. The rocks were slippery. Persis had to hop on one foot, and I was little help to her because she was bigger than me.

We reached the river. Like Persis's ankle, it was swollen, making it impossible for us to cross. The ribbon of water that had refreshed our feet a few hours earlier was now a barrier to warmth and safety.

There was nothing we could do but wait for morning. We climbed under the outstretched branches of a large bush, which was little protection against the storm. Persis's ankle began to throb with pain. Dirt and gravel clung to the cuts on her leg.

Thoughts of encountering the buck again kept us from returning to the shelter of the niche in the side of the hill. Persis began to cry. I was glad she did because I'd wanted to cry but was afraid she would think I was a baby. Her crying gave me permission to cry. Huddled against each other we wailed against the booming thunder.

I remember how badly my stomach hurt from fear and worry. What if the buck showed up again? This time there was no place to escape him. And what if there were lions in the area like Rufus and Apelles had said? Stories of lions leaping from the bushes beside the river and mauling full-grown men were common.

Not only was I afraid, I was worried. My thoughts turned to Mother. How frightened she must be for my safety. And even if somehow we managed to live through this ordeal, how disappointed she would be in me. I knew better than to go into the hills. My disobedience hurt not only me, it was hurting her.

I spent the worst night of my life under that bush with Persis, cold and shivering, hungry and scared, drenched to the bone and jumping with fright with every flash of lightning.

In the morning we were found. About twenty men from town came looking for us. To this day I don't know what made them think to look in the hills for us. I was too ashamed and frightened to ask.

And while I was overjoyed at being found, my joy was tempered by thoughts of facing Mother.

Even now it's difficult for me to put into words how relieved I was by her reaction. She embraced me with tears. Not an angry word came from her mouth. Over and over she thanked God for watching over me. For some reason I couldn't stop shivering.

Mother stripped off my drenched, soiled clothes and bundled me in a clean blanket. Then, though it had been years since she held me like that, she cradled me in her lap. I curled into a ball and snuggled against her. She began humming. I could feel the music echoing in her chest.

There was a moment between sleep and consciousness when the ache of that horrible, wretched day disappeared. Wrapped securely in loving arms. Sleepy warm. Calmed by music that penetrates the soul. Do you know what I'm talking about? Now, stretch that feeling into eternity and you have a glimpse of what heaven is like.

Home,
Theodora

# Testimony of a Rich Woman
## Shankala

Beloved,

Wealth was the last thing I expected. Or wanted. A hut that didn't leak, a garden, and a cow—these were sufficient for me. I didn't have time to manage more than this. After all, I'd seen how possessions distracted folks from the Lord and became a source of worry, envy, and unhappiness. Why would I want that?

And since we're being truthful here, the passages in the Scriptures that spoke of wealth in heaven were a bother to me; you knows—like the one that says to lay up treasure in heaven even though you don't have much on earth. And then there was brother John's vision of heaven with all them gems and glitter and crowns and gold, why just the thought of havin' to polish all those gems nearly wore me to a frazzle. It just didn't seem right for a faith that placed such a high value on sacrifice to promise riches in the great beyond.

Didn't our Lord tell the rich young man to sell off all he had? And didn't he praise the woman who gave her last mite at the great temple? And if riches made it harder for folks to get into heaven, why would they be rewarded with riches once they got there?

So when the moment came for the presentation of my heavenly treasure, I wasn't lookin' forward to it. I was led to an area next to the throne room. They told me it was the Treasure Room. It was the largest room I'd ever seen. Pillars were so tall they stretched—well, I can't say they stretched to the heavens since that's where I was standin'—let's just say I'd never seen pillars so tall in all my born days. And the room stretched into forever too. The other side was so far away, I could barely make out the fancy stuff on the walls.

I remember thinking how unnecessary it all was. I was a simple woman. Just give me a hut that didn't leak, a garden, and a cow, and I'd be happy. I don't need none of that other stuff.

Then the people started comin'. Why they poured in from between the pillars on every side and just kept on a comin'. Smiling. Laughing. Pointing at me and whispering to one another. People of all ages, from all countries. Was I so odd looking that they'd all come to see me?

And they kept comin' until that whole room was filled and they still came! They bunched around the pillars and out into the street.

Then, they paraded in front of me—entire families, mothers and children, young people, old people, of tribes and villages and countries I didn't recognize. One by one they introduced themselves, smiling and crying at the same time. Hugging my neck. Blessin' me. Telling their children what a wonderful Christian woman I was.

Let me tell you, it was overwhelming and embarrassing all at the same time. Because I didn't knows a one of them.

Finally I had to say something. In as loud a voice as I could manage, for the room was very large, I thanked them all, but said that I didn't deserve any of this, that I was just a poor woman from an Ethiopian village and they must have mistaken me for someone important.

A silence fell over the whole room.

Then, a little girl—a precious young thing, bright and alert—said to me in an innocent voice, "But we're your treasure."

"My treasure?" I still didn't understand.

Everyone was nodding. "We're your treasure," the girl's father confirmed. "If it hadn't been for you, none of us would be here."

Well, I looked at him hard and long, but truth be told, I had never seen the man before in my life. Now I knew they'd mistaken me for someone else.

"No mistake," the man said. "You're Shankala from the Wallamo province in Ethiopia, and a daughter of the King of kings."

That was my name. And I was from Wallamo. But this was the first time I'd been called a daughter of the King. It sounded good. But still I was puzzled. How could they all know me and I not knows them?

The man spoke again. "Most of us are a product of the great revival in the Damota district," he said.

"I've heard of the revival," I said, "but it was miles and miles from my home. I had nothin' to do with it."

He smiled. "Over ten thousand people were added to the Kingdom during that revival," he said. "And hundreds of thousands more through the families and preachers and missionaries who trace their spiritual roots back to that revival."

"Now I'm sure there is some mistake," I said. "I was never in the Damota district."

But that man was a persistent one. He just kept on smilin' at me. Everyone did. Like there was a secret and everyone know'd it but me.

"Five preachers were used by the Spirit during that revival," he said. He named them.

I'd never heard of a one of them.

"They came from the church started in the home of Chormo and Pakarei."

I looked at him quizzically.

"A man and wife who lived in Damota."

A couple stepped forward. He had his arm around her shoulders. They were smilin' as they greeted me in the Lord as though we were lifelong friends. I returned their greeting.

"They came to the Lord through Biru," the man said.

At last, a familiar face stepped forward! I'd seen this man, though I couldn't remember from where. He wasn't a resident of Wallamo and I didn't remember doin' business with him, only his face was familiar to me.

"My brother is Garmana," Biru said.

"Of course! Garmana," I cried, making the family connection. Garmana was an outspoken member of our village against Christianity. He openly berated the missionaries and everything they wanted to do in Wallamo.

"We were never introduced," Biru said, "but we have a mutual friend."

There was a parting of people. A young man stepped forward.

"Jaldo!" I cried. He was older and taller than I remembered him. But there was no mistaking his grin.

Jaldo greeted me in the Lord. "You remember me," he said.

"Of course I remember you!" It was now my turn to explain to the others. "When my arms and legs grew old and stiff, I used to hire Jaldo to work my garden for me. The missionaries recommended him. He's a fine Christian young man."

Jaldo beamed.

"So now you understand," said the man with the little girl.

I looked at Jaldo. It was so good to see him in God's Kingdom, but I had to confess that I still didn't understand what all these people had to do with me.

Jaldo spoke. "Remember when Garmana's hut burned down?" he asked.

I remembered. As usual in such cases, all the men of the village came together to raise another one in its place. They brought straw and poles to assist in the building. And, as was the custom in Wallamo, Garmana would provide the beer for the men to drink. This was a dilemma for the men in Wallamo who became Christians. They wanted to help their neighbors, but their new beliefs wouldn't allow them to drink the beer during the hut-raisin'. This angered the non-Christian men in Wallamo. When they got drunk, they would beat the Christian men. The Christians stopped going to hut-raisin's where beer was served.

Jaldo didn't think this was right. He wanted to help Garmana build his house, but he was afraid that if he didn't drink beer, he would be beaten. He was agonizing over his decision while working in my garden.

"Do you remember what you told me?" he asked.

In truth, I didn't remember.

169

"You said, 'It is never wrong to do the right thing. God will make you strong.'"

I remembered now.

"Jaldo attended the house-raisin'," Biru continued. "As he feared, several of the men grew angry when he refused to drink with them. He explained that it was wrong for him to drink beer since becoming a Christian. They made fun of him. Played jokes on him. And on his way home that night they beat him."

Jaldo smiled at the telling, the pain of the beating long forgotten.

Biru said, "To see a young man so strong in his convictions impressed me. I wanted to know more about this Jesus who gave him such courage. So I hired him to work for me. He took me to his church and soon I was a Christian too."

"God called him to preach," Jaldo said of Biru proudly.

Biru nodded. "And He provided me with a hard worker in Jaldo to care for my farm so I could have the freedom to travel about preaching."

There was a pause as they all stared at me, grinnin' proudly.

"All because of you," said the man with the little girl.

"Your words gave me the courage to go to the house-raisin'," Jaldo said.

"And Jaldo's example made me curious about Jesus and led to my salvation and call to ministry," Biru said.

"And Biru's preaching led us to the Lord," Chormo said.

"So we started a Bible study, which produced five preachers who the Spirit used to start a revival in Damota," his wife Pakarei added.

"Which sparked a revival that saved ten thousand souls," said the man with the little girl, "the children and grandchildren and great-grandchildren of which continue to do things that advance the Kingdom of God."

"See?" said the little girl. "We're your treasure."

I never thought I'd be comfortable with wealth. But now that I knows the extent of my treasure, I have to say I enjoy bein' a wealthy woman. And to think it all started with an investment I never even remembered making.

The wealthy,
Shankala

# 32

# Dirty Socks
## Jared

Loved ones,
   It was late afternoon. LAX airport was a zoo. I was returning from Atlanta following a disappointing meeting with television executives and all I could think about was getting home. Me and a thousand other people.
   The lines to board flights stretched past the metal detectors. People were camped out all over the floor. If I wasn't high-stepping over someone, I was elbowing my way upstream to baggage claim.
   The crowd thinned a bit. I broke into a narrow clearing and accelerated to a near run. At the other end of the clearing, coming straight at me, was a skycap pushing an elderly woman in a wheelchair. We eyed each other. One of us would have to yield.
   Just then the woman shouted, "Stop!"

The skycap pulled up. He leaned over the back of the wheelchair to check his passenger. Everyone within earshot was looking at her too.

A frail arm lifted. She was pointing at something. We looked to see what it was. Just beyond a huge window the sky was ablaze with brilliant orange light as the sun gave a final sigh and slipped quietly beneath the horizon.

"Good work, God!" the woman shouted.

Instantly, the atmosphere in the airport changed. There were smiles. Steps were lighter. Such is the power God's creation has on our emotions.

I must confess, in my earthly existence I was one of those guys who jumped into his SUV every chance I could and fled the city. The beach, the mountains, the lake, the river, the desert, you name it. I loved the outdoors.

It always amused me that people claimed to love God's creation, yet spent so little time enjoying it themselves, preferring to pay writers and photographers to enjoy it for them and record the experience. *National Geographic* specials, for instance, and the Travel Channel. Over 425,000 people paid to have Arizona Highways delivered to their door so they could gaze at the wonders of creation from an armchair.

Every time we sang Carl Boberg's great hymn in church I wanted to rewrite the words so that people wouldn't lie when they sang it.

O Lord, my God, when I in awesome wonder
Consider all the beauty on this page.
I see the stars as I nod off in slumber,
Thy power throughout this magazine displayed.

So it should come as no small surprise to you that many of my favorite Scripture passages come from

David's pen. Particularly a psalm recorded in the book of Deuteronomy.

The setting was this: The Ark of the Covenant, which had been lost to the Philistines during a time of great corruption, had been returned to Israel but remained at the city of Keriath-Jearim. This was during the reign of King Saul. Not until David gained the throne was the Ark brought back to Jerusalem amid great rejoicing. During the celebration the king led God's people in a celebration of praise. In a song he wrote for the celebration, he called on all the nations of the earth to join creation in praising God.

> Let the heavens be glad, and let the earth rejoice: and let men say among the nations, The LORD reigneth. Let the sea roar, and the fullness thereof: let the fields rejoice, and all that is therein. Then shall the trees of the wood sing out at the presence of the LORD, because he cometh to judge the earth. O give thanks unto the LORD; for he is good; for his mercy endureth for ever.
>
> 1 Chronicles 16:31–34

David had a way with words, didn't he?

I love the way he put it—Don't stop the sea from roaring. Don't stop the trees from singing out at the presence of the Lord. He pointed out that creation doesn't need to be reminded to praise God. It does it naturally. Of all creation, man is the holdout. And not only do we not praise God, we tend to do things that prevent nature from doing what it does naturally.

His message to us? Don't stop creation from praising God; instead, lift up your voice, O ye nations, and join it!

It's one of the few heavenly activities you can enjoy on earth. This is one area where the future Kingdom and the present Kingdom intertwine.

When I first made this realization in life, I decided I could use a little more heaven on earth, so I began looking for ways to praise God.

I turned off the television, choosing to experience life firsthand rather than watching it parade before me on a blue-tinted screen. I exchanged the sound of squealing tires in chase scenes and the barrage of "this will make you happy" advertisements and the screams of terrorized victims and the rat-a-tat-tat of automatic weapons for the reality of God's Kingdom in creation.

I took my family to the top of Mt. Palomar to gaze at the blackness of space and marvel at the milky band of our galaxy. I would wake them up early to see the sunrise, and as a family we would sit and watch the sunset. Have you ever noticed that sunrises and sunsets are painted with different hues? My elementary school daughter pointed that out to me.

We went to the forest to listen to the wind whistle in the treetops while the rustling leaves and groans and pops of the tree trunks provided background percussion.

It was then that I realized we were confining our enjoyment to things we could see and hear. So we began to look for ways to worship God through His creation with all five of our senses.

We stood on the beach and felt the ocean breeze wash over our faces and leave our skin tingly and tasting of salt.

We baked our own bread just so we could taste grain fresh from the oven.

We went to the snowcapped peaks and filled our lungs with crisp air in the early winter and stripped off layers of clothing to enjoy the summer sun warming our bodies.

With each of these experiences we joined the sunflowers in lifting our faces heavenward in praise to God.

Then God spoke to me. It was a stunning revelation, one that came to me while listening to a radio sermon on the way home from the studio one night. The passage was from the book of Romans. *For we know that the whole creation groaneth and travaileth in pain together until now* (Rom. 8:22).

I couldn't help but wonder why God's wondrous creation that had become so much a part of our spiritual lives was groaning. The next verse explained it. Like us, it was waiting for its redemption, because it too has been bruised by sin.

The radio preacher went on to explain how sin has warped all of God's creation. He said it was as though a vandal broke into a sculptor's studio and placed his hands on the still-fresh clay bust of a man's face and twisted it. While the bust would still have humanlike features—a nose, a mouth, eyes—it would be a distorted representation of the man it was designed to portray.

That's when it hit me. This wondrous creation of God, this creation that can take our breath away, this creation that can leave us humbled by its majesty, is a sin-warped creation. Even in all its beauty, it's a twisted, marred representation of God's original handiwork. In other words, compared to what God has in store for us when creation is redeemed, this present universe has all the appeal of a pair of dirty socks.

Then, in horror, it dawned on me what it took to make this redemption possible. The Creator Himself had to suffer at the hands of His own creation. He allowed the rebellious lumps of clay that had been animated by His breath to seize Him, try Him, and sentence Him to die. He struggled up a hill called Calvary that He fashioned with His own hands. Stripped and naked, He was fixed to a cross with nails made from ore He composed and hid in the hills. He hung on that cross made from trees He planted and nourished and watered.

This He did to redeem all creation. His eyes closed that we might see the light. His ears were encased in a silent tomb that we might hear the angels sing. His lungs collapsed that we might breathe as free people. His tongue was stilled and swollen that we might taste heaven's glory. His fingers grew cold and stiff that we might touch the face of God.

Creation, the sequel. Coming soon.

Still praising after all these years,<br>
Jared

# 33

# Ordinary Heroes
## Shankala

Beloved,

When I was just a youngun' my mother told me stories of tribes long, long ago. One of the stories was about a tribe that was being terrorized by a lion. He was no longer king of a pride, which meant he had to do all of his huntin' himself since he had no females to hunt for him. As he had grown old, he was no longer cunning and swift of foot. In order for him to survive he preyed upon cattle and the little children of the village.

The men of the village knew what they had to do. The lion had to be hunted down and killed. They grabbed their spears and set out to find and kill the lion. All except one man. He didn't join the huntin' party because he was afraid.

A few days later, the hunters returned, dragging the carcass of the dead lion behind them. Everyone in the village came out for the celebration. The children were no longer afraid. They danced around the lion. The bravest of them ran up and touched the dead animal.

In the midst of the great celebration, the coward emerged from his hut. He strode toward the lion all tall and bravelike and, when he was certain everyone was looking, he kicked it.

So it is with all peoples and cultures. Some people sees what needs to be done and does it, and then there are the dead lion kickers.

Dr. Parker already told you about how we are a cloud of witnesses. We gets to see acts of courage that are as exciting as Daniel in the lion's den, and acts of such great cowardice that the angels weep. But we're always waiting for the next great act of godly courage. The telling of it sets the whole place to jumpin'.

Brother Jared had an interesting comment on the subject. He said that in his earthly country when people were asked to name their heroes, they listed people who played games or actors and actresses who play-acted heroic roles in dramas. We found that amusin'.

As you might suppose, we have lots of real heroes here in heaven. And I must confess to you that when I crossed through the veil the thought of seeing any of the great heroes of faith unnerved me.

Then I thought to myself, "Self, who is you kiddin'?" Brother Abraham is going to have one of the finest mansions in heaven, none finer I imagine, and my hut will surely be on the far edge of the village somewhere. And Moses, who escorted the children out of Egypt and went to the mountaintop to bring down the stones of law; and David, the great king who had God's own heart and who wrote all those powerful songs; and brother Paul who took the message of God from city to city, and who got stoned for doin' it, yet who still found time to write such pretty words about love; and brother Enoch who walked so close beside God he just sorta straggled into heaven—all of them will most certainly be in a special part of heaven reserved for the great and mighty with plenty of *No Trespassin'* signs all over the place. So I never expected to bump into any of them no matter how long eternity was.

I was pleased enough to meet the likes of Charles McCleary, a missionary man of God who took the Word of God to West Africa and who died of fever six months after returning to Elat following a trip home. While he was there he told the church that sent him that when a bridge is built, some foundation stones must be laid beneath the water and that if God willed it, he was willin' to be one of those stones, laid out of sight yet providing a foundation for the others. And sure enough, he was. His widow continued his work, and the Elat church became a gatherin' place for the gospel for the whole region. And a nicer young man and prettier wife you'd ever care to meet.

After getting to know them, you knows what they did? They said, "Come with us, we want to introduce you to some of our neighbors." I nearly dropped my teeth when I saw who their neighbors was.

Moses. And King David, who is still singing those pretty songs of his. And brother Paul, who is now rested after all that walkin' he did on earth. And Abraham and Sarah, what a lovely couple.

And they all chatted with me just like I was somebody! And, oh, the stories they tell! So many of them that aren't recorded in the Holy Scriptures. And they laughed and listened to each other—and listened to me! They wanted to know all about my life and my earthly walk with Jesus. I told them the story about the dead lion kicker.

Then, do you knows what King David said about me? He said that he was glad to meet such a courageous woman!

'Course I knew he was just bein' polite, and I told him so. He insisted and Moses agreed with him. But I just shook my head and said, "I'm not anyone special. All I did was try my best not to make my Lord ashamed of me."

And King David said, "Exactly. That's why you're a hero."

I never thought myself a hero. And still didn't. King David—he has the ability to look into your eyes and knows what you're thinkin'—he said, "A hero is an ordinary person who knows what he believes and is willing to stand up for what he believes no matter who stands against him."

All the others nodded their agreement.

Then Moses said, "It's an honor for us to meet heroes like you and missionary McCleary."

Well, what a day that was. I'll never forget it, that's for sure. And I still don't think I'm a hero like they said, but I tell you one thing I learned about them—when we was sitting around talkin', they talked just like ordinary people, though we all knows they did some extraordinary things.

As for me and for all those good things they said 'bout me, I knows they was just bein' nice.

An ordinary woman,<br>
Shankala

# 34

# When Heaven Was Helpless

## Jared

Loved ones,

One of the joys of being at home is the clarity of vision. Spiritual things that we once had to take by faith are now readily visible to us. The blinders have been removed from our eyes. We see the promise given to Nathanael—angels ascending and descending, doing the work of the Lord.

The Bible gives us a glimpse of these things—visitations to Zecharias and Joseph and Mary, the heavenly host announcing Jesus' birth, the stirring of the pool at Bethesda, the Apostle Peter's jailbreak—these things always struck me as special occurrences of the interaction between the divine and the human. What has struck me most since coming home is the regularity with which interaction with angels takes place.

And if you want a truly different perspective on things, talk to an angel. They have a cosmic view of events that casts all of human history in a totally different light.

Talking with angels this way reminds me of radio commentator Paul Harvey and his unique style of relating events that occurred "behind the scenes" of the news stories. At the end of each segment, he would say, "And now you know the rest of the story." Well, listening to the stories of angels is like listening to Paul Harvey—you get to hear "the rest of the story."

One of my favorites is hearing about the time Lucifer requested an audience with God and made his charge against Job. Needless to say, tensions were high. Many of the angels present had been among those Lucifer had unsuccessfully attempted to recruit to his side. They knew firsthand what he could do.

To place the reputation of heaven on the shoulders of one man was a bold challenge. And then for the Father to accept the challenge! Well, let's just say God had more faith in people than the angels did. They fully expected Him to protect His favorite. But God knew Job's heart, and Job came through with flying colors.

But the time most talked about by the angels was the day God shut heaven down. The day the doors were closed between earth and heaven; the day there was no ascending or descending.

As you might suspect, this had to do with the series of events that was the boldest stroke of all, the stroke that broke Lucifer's back and sealed his fate forever.

The announcement sent shock waves throughout the cosmos when God announced the incarnation. After all, who but God would have thought of such a thing? Who in heaven would have dared stand before the Almighty Presence and say, "Let's take your Son, nail Him to a cross for the sin of humankind." Only God could have come up with such a plan.

Now you need to remember that the angels were accustomed to serving the Lord since before human history, especially during the act of creation. To think of Jesus encased in flesh was beyond comprehension.

They watched in horror as He lay aside His perfect knowledge and as He stripped Himself of His radiant glory. They wept for years to see Him reduced to the form of a man. Though they knew it was the Father's will, it was difficult for them to look at Him in such an emaciated state of existence.

To them the plan was brilliantly painful to watch unfold. Of course, they were given their assignments: Gabriel to inform Mary and Zecharias, the heavenly host to announce the King's coming to the shepherds. There were always certain angels charged with keeping watch over Him. One was dispatched to care for Jesus following the contest with Satan in the wilderness that had cosmic consequences. Another strengthened Him on the Mount of Olives the night He was betrayed. Twelve legions stood by, ready to rush to His aid. All He had to do was bid them come.

Imagine their dismay when the comforting angel returned from the Mount of Olives to hear the general order from on High suspending all further operations on earth until further notice. The Prince was on His own. The heavenly host stood by, helpless as they watched the Son cursed, beaten, abused, and killed.

Gabriel. Michael. The legions of heaven. Restricted to base, so to speak.

To attempt to minimize their agony by saying they knew that Jesus would be raised from the dead is to speak from ignorance. If you think the angels obeyed this noninterference command easily, you don't understand free will and the cosmic conflict. The shadow of the cross fell darkly across the heavens, and with it came temptations to doubt, rebel, and revolt.

The Glory of Heaven handed over to a rebellious creation. The sinless Son of God suffering the agony of torn flesh and collapsed lungs. The beloved Son seeing His Father turn His back on Him. The Eternal One trudging into the muck of Hades and death.

This is what they were forced to witness. Any one of them could have rescued him. But they didn't.

That day has left its mark on the angels. There is no objectivity when it comes to sin among the ranks of the angels. They who have resisted the call to rebellion themselves have little patience with humans who side with evil. They who knew the Son before He became flesh know all too well the price that was paid for salvation.

Of course, the ban on earth was lifted. And as before, the angels are ascending and descending as they perform their various tasks. There are preparations for Jesus' return to earth. The list of those who will accompany Him is long. And while the time of His return has been kept from them, they talk about it. They anticipate the day when every knee shall bow.

As you might expect, there are rumors. Any day they expect to hear the sound of the trumpet that will announce His return. Just this morning one of the heavenly host nudged me and said, "Have you heard? Gabriel is licking his lips."

And now you know the rest of the story,
Jared

# 35

# What Does God Really Want?
## Theodora

Beloved,

A friend of mine was going through a difficult time in her spiritual life. She was feeling unworthy and unloved. At one point, she threw up her hands and shouted, "Just what does God want from me anyway?"

Have you ever noticed that the best questions are asked out of desperation?

What *does* God want from us?

One thing I've learned, the answer to this doesn't change regardless of which side of the veil you're on. God wants the same from us here in the fullness of the Kingdom as He wants from you who are still journeying on earth. However, we have a distinct advantage on this side of the veil—when God smiles, we can see it.

So then, from our experiences here, what makes God smile?

Let me put it this way, when you love someone you want to make them happy, don't you? You find out their favorite places and take them there. You find out what they like to eat and prepare it for them. You find out what makes them laugh, because there's nothing better than seeing someone you love laughing.

When God is pleased, His smile could light a thousand dawns. And what will provoke that smile?

His Son, Jesus. A prouder Father you will never see. God repeatedly expressed His pleasure in His son during Jesus' days on earth: *And a voice came from heaven: "You are my Son, whom I love; with you I am well pleased"* (Mark 1:11).

If God the Father wore buttons they'd be busting every day. He loves showing His Son off: *God . . . was pleased to reveal his Son in me so that I might preach him among the Gentiles* (Gal. 1:15–16).

And it pleased God that His plan of redemption for humankind worked to perfection: *For God was pleased to have all his fullness dwell in him, and through him to reconcile to himself all things, whether things on earth or things in heaven, by making peace through his blood, shed on the cross* (Col. 1:19–20).

And it pleases Him still whenever people hear the word of the gospel and discover His plan of redemption for them: *God was pleased through the foolishness of what was preached to save those who believe* (1 Cor. 1:21).

So God is mighty pleased when He sees His work of redemption through His Son working to perfection like it has been down through the ages. He loves to hear people talking about His Son, Jesus. He loves hearing the gospel preached. He loves bringing new people into the Kingdom day by day. These are the things that bring a smile to His face more often than anything else.

But there's one thing more. More than anything else, God breaks into a smile when one of His children comes home.

God loves to see the expression on His children's faces when they first step through the veil. When they first realize that all of His promises are true. When they see Jesus face-to-face. When they see the gathering of their loved ones waiting for them. When they feel the lack of fear and pain and realize it's a permanent condition. When they see life the way He's always intended it to be.

It brings a smile to His face every time.

Until then, what does God want from you? He wants you to live as though you believe the Kingdom is really yours.

*"Do not be afraid, little flock, for your Father has been pleased to give you the kingdom"* (Luke 12:32).

Waiting for you beyond the veil,<br>
Theodora

# The Lamb Standing
## Shankala

Beloved,

Sometimes life is so hard you just wants to sit in the ashes with brother Job and cut yourself and wail. Flapping-lip explanations by well-meanin' friends are less than helpful, they're annoying. There is no reasoning at times like this. The pain is too great. So great, you don't knows if you can bear it.

The day we heard the news of Tommy Devers's death was one of those times. Tommy was one of them missionaries that taught us 'bout God. He didn't have to come to our land, mind you. But God said, "Go," and Tommy said, "Yes, Lord."

He left his land and his family. He showed us pictures of them. We called them the smilin' family because they all had grins just like his. Tommy was tall and as thin as a tent pole, but somehow God managed to squeeze into him a wide love. No other missionary taught us more about the joy of bein' in Christ than Tommy.

We couldn't believe it when we heard that Tommy had been killed in the Dassi Desert. He was traveling to a different camp to tell them about the love of God when he came upon a band of Arussies, an old tribe that still practices the old ways. Among the Arussies, before a man is allowed to marry, he must prove his manhood by killin' another man. Proof of the killin' is required—his victim's male organs. The men they kill usually bleed to death.

Even now (I talked with Tommy before writing this letter and asked his permission to tell you his story), I cannot find the words to tell you how deeply the news of Tommy's death hurt me and all the others in the village. It hurt knowin' that this good man did not deserve to be killed like this by savage men. And it hurt knowin' that we would no longer hear his teaching about God's love or see him walkin' and smilin' among our children in the village.

There is a heaviness that comes with tragic news, a heaviness that weakens the knees and clouds the mind with grief and drains the soul of joy. Food becomes tasteless. Conversation is nothin' more than irritating noise. And life loses its meaning. What could be worse?

Well, how about if you was the one responsible for someone else's death? Would that be worse?

I told you I spoke to Tommy before writing this letter. I also talked with three others—each of them was responsible for someone's death.

One was a night attendant who worked at a home for elderly people who were unable to care for themselves. He fell asleep. A machine that makes coffee started a fire that killed several of the people he was supposed to be caring for.

Then there was a woman who was drivin' her auto-
mobile and as she backed away from her house, she felt
a bump. When she got out to see what happened, she
found her son's best friend under the wheels. He was
seven years old.

The third was a hunter who had stretched out on a
wire fence for his longtime friend to climb through.
They'd done this hundreds of times for each other. Only
this time the hunter's gun went off accidentally and shot
his friend through the heart.

Can there be any worse feelin' than this? The weight
of this kind of tragedy is unbearable. Who can stand
under it?

I asked each of these good people how they managed
to survive such a horrible ordeal. Do you know what
they told me? They said prayer and belief that God had
a plan, even for this, was what helped them through
such a tough time. In fact, each of them said the accident actually increased their faith in God. It drove them
back to God's Word.

The woman who killed her son's friend told me that
a verse from the prophet Isaiah was 'specially helpful to
her:

But they that wait upon the LORD shall renew their
strength; they shall mount up with wings as eagles; they
shall run, and not be weary; and they shall walk, and not
faint.

Isaiah 40:31

I'll try to explain it to you like she explained it to me.

She said there are some days in life that are so good,
we feel like we're soarin' on eagle's wings. Life couldn't
be better.

191

Most days we're given enough energy for the day. Day after day we do the things that need to be done, and we thank God for our lives. That's like running and not growing weary.

But then, there are days when it seems like we don't even want to wake up in the mornin'. We feel there's no reason to carry on. Life is dark and hopeless. In those days, they who waits upon the Lord renews their strength. Sometimes puttin' one foot in front of the other without fainting is enough. This, too, comes from God.

This is the way I felt when I learned of Tommy Devers's death. It was hard just thinking about goin' on. But you know what helped me most? A picture in my mind. It was a picture from the Bible.

Our brother the Apostle John had painted that picture in the Book of Revelation with the words the Holy Spirit gave him as an encouragement for the believers who were greatly persecuted for their faith. To understand the picture, you've got to know the pictures that came just before it.

First, there was the picture of terrible suffering—war, famine, plagues, martyrs, and the killin' of God's two witnesses. Then there was the picture of a great fiery red dragon chasing after a woman and her child. Then there was the picture of a monstrous beast risin' up out of the sea.

The red dragon and the monstrous beast were a powerful duo. They were a scourge to the Lord's people. These were dark times when nights were long, bellies were empty, sores were plentiful, strength was gone, and hope seemed but a dream. Who could stand in such a day? What hope was there against the fiery dragon and the demonic beast?

And then our brother John wrote, *Then I looked, and there before me was the Lamb, standing on Mount Zion* (Rev. 14:1).

Oh my. What a precious picture that is! The lamb standin' on Mt. Zion.

Let the dragon do his worst. Let the beast roar his loudest. Let the plagues ravage the land and the sores on the people multiply. Standin' in the midst of it all is the unbowed Lamb of God. Triumphant over it all.

That was the picture that kept me strong when I was weakest. Whenever I would lose heart, whenever my pain became unbearable, whenever I felt like sitting in the ashes and wailin', I would close my eyes and see the Lamb standin' on top of His holy hill. Seeing Him standin' there somehow made me strong.

The Lamb's little lamb,
Shankala

# Finding Your Way Home
## Jared

Loved ones,

The phone rang.

It was a friend of my father's whom I hadn't seen in years. He was in Southern California and wanted to stop by and visit me and my family.

It was Saturday. I was in shorts, my legs were covered with grass clippings, and the house was in no condition to entertain guests, but Roy was like family.

"Where are you now?" I asked.

He said he was on Palm Avenue and wanted to know how to get to the house from there. Easy enough. At least so I thought. I gave him directions.

After alerting my wife, I brushed the grass off my legs, put the lawn mower in the garage, and hastily swept the front walk. I was in the bedroom changing shirts when the phone rang again.

"This is Roy. Your directions were no good."

"Where are you?"

"On Thirteenth Avenue. How do I get to your house from here?"

No disaster. Thirteenth Avenue wasn't too far away, but it was a long street. "Where on Thirteenth are you?" I asked.

"I don't know. There's a gas station across from me."

There were hundreds of gas stations on Thirteenth. "What's the nearest cross street?"

"I can't read it from here."

"Okay. What else do you see near you?"

"A library."

A library? There was no library on Thirteenth Street. The nearest public library was five or six blocks away on Mission Avenue. That was no help. "Umm. What else are you near?"

By now Roy was getting exasperated. I could hear it in his voice. I was hoping that one more landmark would help me pinpoint his position.

"I'm near a chicken sandwich shop," he said.

A chicken sandwich shop? That didn't help at all. Sandwich shop. Sandwich shop. No matter how many times I repeated it in my head, I could not remember any place on Thirteenth Street where there was a gas station, a library and a chicken sandwich shop. My hesitation was not going over well on the other end of the line.

"Don't you know your own city?" Roy said. "Look, just drive down Thirteenth Street until you see me."

He hung up.

What choice did I have? I climbed into the car and headed toward Thirteenth Street. I still had no clue as to where I'd find him. Just a few blocks down Thirteenth, there was Roy standing on the sidewalk exactly where he said he would be.

A quick look around and I understood immediately our inability to communicate. We were of two generations and two different cultures. While Roy was speaking country, I was speaking city.

Those who speak country give directions using visible landmarks. "Just keep heading down the road until you come to a giant oak tree and turn left. You can't miss it." Those who speak city want names and numbers. "Head down Thirteenth Avenue for three quarters of a mile. We're at 555 Thirteenth Avenue on the east side of the street next to Meyer's Department Store."

Once I understood this everything made sense. Roy's landmarks? Across the street was a gas station, sure enough. He was calling from a telephone in a strip mall. A sign on a store entrance said, "Video Rental Library." On the next lot was a fast-food location with a poster in the window featuring their sale item, a chicken sandwich. Everything was just as he said. Yet I failed to identify any of these landmarks.

Had he said, Shell gas station, Knight's Family Video, or Kentucky Fried Chicken, I would have known exactly where to find him.

Of course, we had a good laugh over it. But what if more was on the line than just the reuniting of friends? What if the directions were to heaven?

Good news. God is better at communicating than Roy and I. In the olden days God used objects to teach people about their heavenly home. He gave them the tabernacle. It was a location set aside specifically for God's people. It was entered through a gate. Inside it had an altar for sacrifices, a table with shewbread, a lampstand, and a priest to stand between God and men. The focal point of the tabernacle was the Ark of the Covenant with its outstretched angel's wings. This holy place was where God encountered His creation.

In the latter days, God communicated again. This time instead of using cloth and wood and stone, He used flesh and blood to teach us the way into God's presence. It was a new covenant, but there was no mistaking that the new was based on the old. Jesus was the flesh and blood tabernacle.

Just as before, to encounter God you still go through a gate. Jesus said, *"I am the gate; whoever enters through me will be saved"* (John 10:9).

The altar still provides the needed sacrifice to make us worthy to encounter God. John the Baptist pointed to Jesus and said, *"Look, the Lamb of God, who takes away the sin of the world"* (John 1:29).

What about the other features in the tabernacle? Jesus said, *"I am the bread of life"* (John 6:48) and *"I am the light of the world"* (John 9:5).

As for the priest: *We have a great high priest who has gone through the heavens, Jesus the Son of God* (Heb. 4:14).

And when you step into the holy place to worship God, Jesus will be there: Jesus said, *"I and the Father are one"* (John 10:30) and, *"Anyone who has seen me has seen the Father"* (John 14:9).

God's directions are clear. For the children of God, the way home goes through Jesus.

Standing at the door waiting for you,
Jared

# Preparing
# to Come Home

# Of Faith and Fatalities

### Dr. Everett Parker

Beloved,

In the spring of 1861 my eighteen-year-old son, Thad, and several of his friends, in a rush of patriotism, ran off to see the elephant. President Lincoln had issued a call for 75,000 volunteers to put down the armed insurrection of the South. The boy was ripe for action. He'd just been expelled from school for setting a hog loose in the attic of the schoolhouse and had a mind too active to be tilling farmland. So I let him go.

Thad's first letters home were mostly stories of monkeyshines and high jinks as his regiment was given a brief furlough before moving on to training camp. He boasted frequently of going after Jeff Davis's scalp with his newly-issued Enfield rifle. He told his brothers if they were going to join up, they'd better do it soon, because the war wasn't going to last long.

Then Thad saw the elephant—he experienced war firsthand. It was a Sunday morning. His regiment was camped at Shiloh Church. Throughout the day the Rebels made no fewer than a dozen assaults on his position. It was one of the bloodiest battles of the war, with enormous casualties. Thad survived to write to his younger brothers, "Don't join the war. Two months out and you'll be sick to death of it. I think if I get out of this after three years, I will be doing very well." To me, he wrote, "Father, I know you don't think much of war, and you are right. I don't think the North will ever whip the South so long as there is a man left in the South. They fight like wild devils. Every man seems determined to lose the last drop of blood before he gives up. But there's no use talking about it, because we can't end it."

I remember how thankful to God I was to hear Thad was alive, and how pleased I was that the boy was beginning to mature. But for all the death on the battlefield, he still didn't know the worst of it. As a physician, I knew the bitter truth. The casualties suffered at Shiloh and Bull Run and Gettysburg and all the other battlefields combined couldn't compare to the number of casualties resulting from a much greater enemy—contaminated drinking water.

The truth was, more soldiers were killed by disease than by weapons. Typhoid bacteria was the number one killer. It entered the body through the mouth by ingestion, usually contaminated water. It penetrated the intestinal wall and entered the bloodstream. There was a ten to fourteen day incubation period with early symptoms of headache, generalized aching, fever, and restlessness followed by loss of appetite, nosebleeds, cough, and diarrhea. During the second week of fever, a rash of small, rose-colored spots appeared on the stomach and lasted four to five days before fading away. Ulcers formed on the bowel wall causing the patient to hemorrhage internally. Mental confusion and delirium were common. Fatalities were inevitable.

As a soldier Thad had been trained to face a military enemy; as a physician I had a different perspective from which I saw an even greater enemy. And so lies the difference between you and us.

As Christians on earth, you arm yourselves to battle life's visible temptations, while we, from our heavenly perspective, see a much greater enemy that's invisible.

I'm not speaking of demonic forces, at least not in this letter. I'm speaking of a spiritual disease that affects the heart. A healthy spiritual heart is sensitive to the things of God. The diseased heart turns away from the things of God. Eyes that once beheld God's goodness glaze over with indifference; voices that once sang, "Hallelujah!" now cry out, *Is the Lord among us, or not?* (Exod. 17:7).

Spiritual heart disease enters the body through the eyes and ears affecting one's perception. Symptoms include altered judgment, rendering the infected person susceptible to suggestion. Vision is fixed and restricted to images that glitter and mirages that make promises they cannot deliver. After a time the heart becomes hardened. There is a tendency to wander away from the people and places that once filled them with life. Accordingly, the infected persons grow weak and stumble. If gone untreated, fatalities are inevitable.

Every year millions more Christians succumb to hardening of the heart than fall in spiritual battle.

Like most diseases, this one is preventable. The prevention is outlined by the preacher in the Book of Hebrews:

See to it, brothers, that none of you has a sinful, unbelieving heart that turns away from the living God. But encourage one another daily, as long as it is called Today, so that none of you may be hardened by sin's deceitfulness. We have come to share in Christ if we hold firmly till the end the confidence we had at first.

Hebrews 3:12–14

Heart disease prevention includes routine self-examination, daily doses of encouragement, and holding firmly to what you believe.

Unfortunately, most people treat their spiritual health much like they do their physical health; they neglect it until it's too late.

I once read a medical article about a native tribe in South America whose people died at a young age, much younger than the neighboring tribes. This pattern had gone on for so many generations, the tribe came to accept it. The phenomenon intrigued a team of physicians who studied the tribe in the hope of determining why its people died so young.

They discovered insects living in the natives' adobe homes. The bite of these insects injected a toxin that, over a period of years, became fatal. The natives were given several options: One, destroy the insects using an insecticide. Two, tear down their homes and move to another location. Or three, continue to live as they had for generations and die early.

The tribe held a meeting and made their choice. They chose to ignore the insects and go on living as they had always done for generations. They chose short lives and an early death.

The greatest attack on Christians is an invisible one. It is spiritual in nature and germlike in form. It's affect-

204

ing millions of believers and will affect millions more. The good news is that it's preventable. The bad news is that many believers are becoming disillusioned, bitter, and hardened, and little is being done to assist them back to health. And the worst news is that many of you reading this letter are feeling the symptoms of the disease, know how to treat it, but like the South American tribe you will choose to do nothing.

Seeing his people in this spiritually wasted condition, the prophet Jeremiah once cried, *"Is there no balm in Gilead?"* (Jer. 8:22). The Negro spiritualist answered him:

There is a balm in Gilead to make the wounded whole;
There is a balm in Gilead to heal the sin sick soul.

And so there is.

As a footnote, while my son Thad survived the battle of Shiloh, he didn't survive the war. He died at Queen Street hospital from typhoid fever. It was his death that started my volunteer work at military hospitals.

Faithfully yours,
Everett Parker, M.D.

# Malchus's Ear

## Jared

Loved ones,

I just met the most remarkable fellow. His name is Malchus, and his right ear is legendary.

You probably don't remember him, but he was an eye-witness and unwitting participant in the most famous arrest of all time. And the only reason you might have heard of him is because of our brother the Apostle John's love of detail.

As a writer myself, I can appreciate the artistic touches John used in his Gospel. He had a talent for adding little sensory or temporal details that give his readers a feeling of what it was like to be at the events he described. He painted word pictures with the small brush. For him it was detail, always detail. He would tell us it was cold. It was night. It was the tenth hour. It was winter. And the detail in the account of Jesus' arrest . . . where do I begin?

We know where Jesus was arrested: across the Kidron Valley in a garden. We know the time of day: It was night. We know who came for Jesus: Roman soldiers and officers of the chief priest and Pharisees. We know what they were carrying: torches and lanterns and weapons. We know that although the band came to arrest him, Jesus took the initiative when they arrived, that He identified Himself so powerfully that the soldiers drew back, and that He went to extraordinary lengths to let them know He was the one they were looking for so that His disciples might not be harmed.

We know that Peter brought a sword with him even though it was forbidden by law for him to carry a weapon on a feast day. We know that Peter became unnerved and tried to defend Jesus with his sword. We know that he wildly swung his sword, missing a servant's head, yet severing the man's ear. We know it was his right ear. And we even know the name of the servant. You guessed it. Malchus.

Like I said, detail. Glorious detail. Think of it. There are a number of important people in the Bible whose names we don't know. Can anyone tell me the name of the woman at the well? How about the name of the good Samaritan? Or either of the names of the thieves on the cross? But we know Malchus, whose right ear was cut off the night Jesus was arrested and who was the servant of High Priest Caiaphas.

Now that in itself is significant—that he was the servant of the high priest—because just before the soldiers bound Jesus and led Him away, the Master miraculously reattached Malchus's ear.

Malchus himself continues the story from that point. While Jesus was taken to Annas, who was Caiaphas's father-in-law, for initial questioning, Malchus and the others returned to Caiaphas to report. Not a word was spoken among them as they ascended the stone steps to the high priest's house. He was waiting for them.

"Report," Caiaphas asked. "Did they resist?"

All eyes turned to Malchus.

Eventually the entire incident came out. The trial followed, and Jesus was led to Pilate, then to Calvary. But after that night the relationship between the high priest and his servant Malchus was never the same. Every time Malchus entered the room, Caiaphas looked at his right ear and grew silent.

Why do I tell you the story of Malchus's ear? Because for Caiaphas and everyone in his court who heard of the incident in the garden, Malchus's right ear was a reminder to them that the Kingdom of God was among them.

Our Lord once said to them: *"But if I cast out devils by the Spirit of God, then the kingdom of God is come unto you"* (Matt. 12:28). Or if He raises the dead, or teaches the beatitudes, or heals Malchus's ear. All of these are signs that the Kingdom of God has come.

So it is with every age. The world is filled with Kingdom residents. The language of the Kingdom is spoken every time a Kingdom resident utters an encouraging word in Jesus' name. The customs of the Kingdom are seen every time a selfless deed is done or a sacrifice is made. The values of the Kingdom are demonstrated every time someone subordinates himself to a boss, or a wife, or a husband, or a friend—for while these things are despised by the world, they are marks of greatness in the Kingdom of heaven.

These Kingdom acts are the Malchus's ear of every generation, proof that the Kingdom of God is coming in power. The world is without excuse.

Does this excite you as it does me?

Having been raised in Southern California, I interacted with a cosmopolitan society from my earliest days. I went to school with Hispanics, African Americans, Chinese, Japanese, Filipinos, Jews, and the occasional Englishman or Frenchman. Each had defining characteristics. The younger we were, the less the differences mattered to us. Then, in high school for some reason they became more distinctive.

For some, the characteristics were a matter of identity and pride. For others, it was simply a fact of life that at times provided amusing diversion. For example, on St. Patrick's Day my two best friends, one a Jew, the other a Pole, both dyed their hair red to celebrate my heritage. Quite a sight, let me tell you.

The point that I want to make here is that each of these nationalities are readily recognized by their appearance, language, and culture. Hispanics don't have to go around announcing that there are Hispanics among us; we know it. Even so, those who are Kingdom citizens shouldn't have to go around announcing that the Kingdom is among us; everyone should know it by our appearance, language, and culture.

Our presence should announce that the Kingdom is among us as clearly as Malchus's ear.

Thy Kingdom come,
Jared

# The Gift Unshelved
## Theodora

Beloved,

I always imagined myself being one of the followers of Jesus. I would walk among the olive trees pretending what it must have been like to share the company of so many great women—Mary called Magdalene; Mary, the mother of James; Salome; Joanna, the wife of Cuza, the manager of Herod's household; Susanna; and all the others. Imagine to be counted among the women who helped support Jesus out of their own means.

Then there were those women who were nameless, known only by the incident or location in which they encountered the Master. When no one else was around, I used to sit at the edge of our well and pretend to be shocked that a Jewish male would ask a Samaritan woman for a drink, and I'd blush when it became apparent he knew the intimate details of my life.

Other times I'd pretend to struggle in the grip of angry hands as I was forcibly led into the temple and stood before Jesus where He was teaching. My accusers would shame me by publicly proclaiming me an adulterer worthy of being stoned to death according to the Law. And Jesus would come to my rescue by saying, "If any one of you is without sin, let him be the first to throw a stone at her."

But my favorite imaginary pastime when I was young was pretending I was the woman who anointed Jesus' feet at the home of Simon, the former leper.

I would pretend to take the alabaster jar down from a high shelf and, without introduction and in the full view of all who had gathered for the Passover meal, I'd kneel at the feet of the Master and break the jar. The essence of sweet oil would fill the room. With great tenderness I'd take a shattered portion of the jar that held a measure of oil and I'd anoint the Master's head.

The disciples would scream at me. Jesus would be just as quick to defend me. "Let her alone!" He'd say. "She has done a good thing for Me. She has done what she could. I tell you the truth, wherever the gospel is preached throughout the world, what she has done will also be told, in memory of her." Then I'd stick my nose in the air and strut right in front of those disciples out of the room.

What can I say? I was young.

In spite of my snobbish exit, the incident proved to be a model for me in my earthly life. One day I began thinking about what the Master said in the woman's defense. "She has done what she could." It seemed such a little thing, to do what you can. What other possibilities were there?

She could have withheld her gift. Jesus didn't ask for it. No one was expecting her to use the oil on that occasion. It was as though she walked into the room where the jar of oil was on the shelf, saw it and thought of Jesus. The act that earned such lofty praise from the Master consisted of taking what she had and using it for Him.

She also could have spent her time wondering what great things she could do for Jesus if she was the wife of a rich landowner, or an influential Pharisee, or an exotic queen like the legendary Sheba. All the while her great imaginings would be drawing attention away from the alabaster jar of oil she had on her shelf, which she could use but didn't.

Instead, she did what she could.

The lesson made me take a good hard look at my own life and wonder if there were things I could use to serve the Master, if there were things I could do that I wasn't doing.

And then I got to thinking of the reaction of the disciples and grew angry with them. What business was it of theirs in the first place? Yet it seemed that their reaction was common even in my own church. There seemed to be a maxim at work: No good work goes uncriticized.

It seems as soon as someone starts to do something to serve the Lord, there are a host of others who can think of ways they could have done it better. I wonder if the woman would have brought out the jar if she knew beforehand that this was the reaction she would get from them?

Every time I think of Jesus' reaction, I want to shout with Him, "Leave her alone!"

From the woman with the jar of oil, I learned not to be overly concerned with what other people said about what I did for Jesus. I was doing it for Him, not them.

It became something of a game for me to look at things in our house and to try to match them up with Jesus. I'd look at things and ask, "How could I use that for Jesus?"

The truth behind the teaching was quite liberating. Jesus wasn't asking me to give Him things I didn't have, to do what I couldn't do, to go where I couldn't go. All He was doing was asking me to use what I had.

My possessions.

My talents.

My spiritual gifts.

My time.

To take them down from the shelf, dust them off, break them at His feet and anoint His head with them.

I could do that.

Your friend and sister in the Lord,
Theodora

# The Great Mystery
**Jared**

Loved ones,

There's a great mystery in life. It's the mystery of Christian believers who always expect to get something from a church when they never put anything into it. The principle of something for nothing doesn't work in other aspects of life, so what makes them think it works that way in churches?

Take my brother, for example. Great guy. But his strength is not in accounting, especially when it comes to his checking account. Whenever he wants money, he goes to an ATM machine, pulls a query and if there is money in his account he withdraws it regardless of whether he has outstanding checks.

One time he went to an ATM machine and slipped his card into the slot. The machine ate his card and closed up in his face. It was the bank's way of saying it was tired of the way he was handling his account.

He was violating a basic principle. You can't withdraw money from a banking account unless you've already

214

deposited money into the account. You can't take out something you haven't already put in.

It's a law of nature.

Part of the wisdom of God's timing in revealing Scripture to man is that He chose to do it when the world was largely agricultural. There are so many principles that hold true for crops as they do for all of life. This thought so intrigued me, I once put together a set of these laws for a Bible study lesson. I'd like to share them with you.

**Law One: Not Every Seed Will Produce Fruit.**

This law is for all those who say, "Well I tried being friendly once, and it didn't work." Not every seed produces a bountiful harvest. Some never take root. Some are eaten by birds. Some fall by the wayside. But that doesn't mean that the law of the harvest is broken. From the beginning of time the law has been, you plant seed, you get a harvest.

There was a woman in our church who was one of the most miserable creatures I've ever known. Not only was she miserable, but she seemed to make it her life's goal to make others miserable. My wife, being the sensitive soul she is, tried to break through the woman's crusty exterior. In a moment of rare vulnerability, the miserable woman confessed that she opened herself up to a friend once and that friend hurt her deeply. She said she would never let that happen again. The seed of friendship didn't bear fruit in that instance, so she decided she would never plant in that field again. She died miserable and alone, a woman without any close friends.

What a pity. She should have trusted the law of the harvest.

**Law Two: There Is No Instant Harvest.**

I lived in a day of instant everything. As a young boy I remember Mom fixing us instant mashed potatoes

215

from a box. They had a funny taste to them and just barely resembled potatoes, but we didn't mind because they were instant.

Well, the desire for instant things has carried over into the rest of our lives, including relationships. But for some things there is no instant harvest.

The farmer sows and waits. Cultivates and waits. Waters and waits. He knows the harvest will come at the right time. The same is true for spiritual things. God is in no hurry. He has all the time in the world. Literally. And neither should we be in a hurry. The harvest is worth the wait.

**Law Three: The More You Sow, The More You Reap.**

Imagine a farmer planting a single seed and day after day fussing over it until several months later he has one stalk of corn to show for all his labor. Ridiculous.

Well, it's just as ridiculous when people are stingy about the way they sow seeds of goodwill and friendship and love. The most fascinating part of this for me is that we have direct control over the size of our harvest. If a farmer wants a crop twice the size as he had the previous year, he buys more land and plants twice the amount of seed.

The same is true for life. If you want twice the number of friends, plant twice the number of seeds of friendship. If you want twice the amount of love returned to you, give away twice the amount of love you normally give. The more you sow, the larger your harvest. It's the law.

**Law Four: When The Harvest Comes Everyone Will Know What You've Planted.**

Contrary to what people think, there are no secrets in life. Everyone knows exactly what kind of person you are by the harvest you reap.

I once heard a story about a boy who wanted to go to the watering hole to swim with his friends. His father said he could go after he finished his chores. A sack of seed needed to be planted in the field.

The boy had a bright idea. He dug a hole and dumped all the seed into it. He then ran to tell his father he was going to go swimming.

"Did you plant that whole sack of seed?" his father asked.

"Every last grain," the boy said.

Well, you know what happened. When the seed began to grow, the boy's deception became evident to all.

In like manner, can you imagine a farmer going to harvest his crop only to be surprised by what was growing there?

"I planted corn, and strawberries grew!"

Ridiculous.

You plant corn, you get corn. You plant potatoes, you get potatoes. The same is true in life. When the harvest comes in, there are no surprises. Everyone knows what you've planted.

**Law Five: You Can't Reap What You Haven't Sown.**

This brings us back to where we started. Imagine the farmer who went out in October to reap a crop he never planted in March. We'd conclude the man was addled in the brain. How could he possibly expect a harvest when he hadn't planted any seed?

Which brings me back to the great mystery of those who expect to get something out of a church or a relationship of any kind when they haven't put anything into it. I guess I'll never understand where people get such ridiculous expectations.

Confident of the harvest,
Jared

217

# 42

# It's Not about You

## Shankala

Beloved,

I was asked to write this letter. Dr. Parker was the one who suggested it and Jared backed him up. When I told them this letter needed a learned approach, they both said I was the perfect person to write it.

Don't know whether to feel flattered or hornswoggled.

Guess I'll just do what I always do, and that's to do my best and trust that the good Lord will make up for my shortcomings.

The topic they done give me is the everyday life of the modern believer. Do you see now why I thought someone with learnin' would do a better job at addressing this?

The modern believer.

Guess the first thing I'd have to say is that things have changed since the days of the early believers, and not always for the better. I once heard a preacher say, "The difference between us and the early church is that the early church prayed and fasted. We simply pray fast." It's an old joke, but it has teeth.

Truth is, early believers had some insights into God that seem to have been forgotten down through the ages. Take those early Israelites. They was fanatics about washin' things. Especially themselves whenever they came to worship God in the temple. Have you seen a picture of their temple area? There are pools of water all over the place for washin' themselves.

Now these pools had nothin' to do with sin. That's what the sacrifices were for. These pools were all about purity. They had it in their heads that it was important for a person to be pure before they came into the very presence of God. They was careful to respect the purity of God.

That's something that seems to have been lost among worshipers today—preparing oneself to approach the Almighty God. Cleansing the mind and body to worship Him, out of respect for His purity.

Why don't people concern themselves with purity anymore when it comes to worshiping God? Well, I thinks maybe it's because they're mistaken about the purpose of worship.

They thinks it's about them, but it's not.

They goes lookin' to gets something out of worship rather than to give something in worship. They walks out of the worship service judging it by the measuring stick of their own wants—whether or not they got something out of it or not, whether or not there was something in the preacher's message for them or not, whether the singing was to their likin' or not. They gots it all backwards.

It's not about you.

Worship is about God. Comin' to Him with praise on our lips and counting it a privilege to do so. Comin' to

Him with tithes from our work, and thanking Him for the increase. Comin' to Him simply because He is.

God is.

He exists.

Worship is to remind us that He is. And that He is a holy God. There is no other like Him. And He is a pure God and that's why we ought to come to Him clean and pure, not likes we was comin' out of some sort of favor to Him.

And then there was that early church. You know, the one that met in Jerusalem during the time the Holy Spirit swept down upon them and so confounded them with a glimpse of heaven, then scattered them to the far places of the world with the wonder of God still shining on their faces.

The teachings of the early apostles was plain. If you wanted to learn the ways of the one true God, you prayed and read the Scriptures and meditated on what they said. They were men and women known for their long times of solitude, on their knees so much that they began to resemble camel's knees. They were people who sacrificed for others through frugal living and fasting. They had servants' hearts.

They lived to serve the Kingdom, not be served by the Kingdom.

Here again, the difference between early believers and modern believers is clear. They didn't live as if the church was there to serve them.

It wasn't about them.

It was about God, and they knew it.

The Kingdom, the church, life—it's not about you.

If I was to describe the church on earth today, I'd have to conclude that it's a confederation of thousands of kingdoms. Believers live as though they're kingdoms unto themselves. Churches live as though they're kingdoms unto themselves. Everyone thinks it's about them. But it's not.

It's about God.

It always has been.

And some day the veil that separates the here and the hereafter will be torn in two—just like that ole earthly one was torn on the day Christ died. And everyone will see God for who He is. And everyone will realize how foolish they've been.

There will be no doubt on that day. Everyone will know it's not about them.

It's about God.

It always has been and always will be.

Blessed are the people who understand that on your side of the veil. They won't be surprised. They'll feel right at home, because they'll have been livin' the right way all along.

I don't know what it will take to get present-day believers to understand this. But I'll tell you this: We're looking forward to the day when you understand the glory of God. It's an amazing revelation.

Some of you already knows that. So you knows what I'm talkin' about when I tell you that we're sad of heart until it's clear to everyone. Let me help you get started.

When you go to worship God this week, enter the place of worship with this thought: "It's not about me. It's about God."

To God be the glory,
Shankala

# 43

# A Day's March Nearer Home

## Jared

Loved ones,

Knowing this will be my final letter to you, I've tried to come up with a thought that is worthy of a closing letter. While I don't know whether I've found a worthy thought, I have come up with some parting words: Given the nature of time, every day you're that much closer to home.

I remember having a few Navy friends who, when their enlistment time was running out, would walk around the base shouting "Short!" because their time was short.

So is yours.

Make your days count.

Each day you live, each breath you take, each moment, each heartbeat means you are one step closer to home.

Some are closer than others. Our brother Frederick Myconius was just telling me about his time on earth when he was deathly ill. Everyone, including himself, expected that he would die within a short time. Accordingly, he said his good-byes to those loved ones who were nearby, and he took up his pen to write a few notes to those he loved who were distant.

When one of his friends received the letter Frederick had sent him, he sat down immediately and drafted a reply in which he said, "I command thee in the name of God to live, because I still have need of thee. The Lord will never let me hear that thou art dead, but will permit thee to survive me. For this I am praying, this is my will, and may my will be done, because I seek only to glorify the name of God."

By the time Frederick received this reply, he had already lost his ability to speak. But within days of receiving the letter, he showed marked improvement and was soon well again. He had work to do.

As for the friend who prophesied Frederick's recovery, Frederick did indeed survive him by two months. And when Frederick finally stepped through the veil into the undiluted Kingdom, there was Martin Luther, his friend, to greet him with tears. For while the work of the Reformation in Europe was great, it was clear to both of them now what Luther had asked of his friend. To forgo the Kingdom for even a brief time to further the work on earth was a sacrifice the likes of which neither could imagine at that time.

But Frederick did not regret his extended stay in the body, for it did indeed glorify God. And, after all, that is our foremost goal no matter on which side of the veil we dwell.

To God be the glory, forever and ever. Amen.

So then, whether you are within arm's reach of the veil that separates us, or decades away, I would encourage you to live your days proudly as a citizen of the Kingdom until God calls you home.

If I were to summarize what we have tried to convey to you with these letters, I would have to call upon Scripture:

> Do not conform any longer to the pattern of this world, but be transformed by the renewing of your mind. Then you will be able to test and approve what God's will is—his good, pleasing and perfect will.
>
> Romans 12:2

Remember who you are. Remember *whose* you are. The moment you were saved, you were born into the Kingdom. You are no longer a citizen of earth or any earthly government. You are a resident and heir of the Kingdom of God. Live as a child of the King until the day you claim your inheritance.

As part of a great cloud of witnesses, I would remind you that there is nothing you face that has not been faced by one of us. We're cheering you on until the day when the full number of God's family has found its way home.

It has been a distinct honor and privilege to write these letters to you. Dr. Parker, Shankala, and Theodora send their love. We await your arrival.

Grace and peace,
Jared